THE
MIRACLE OF
MEDITATION

THE
MIRACLE OF
MEDITATION

Opening Your Life to Peace, Joy, and the Power Within

RYUHO OKAWA

IRH Press

Originally published in Japan as *Meisou No Gokui* by IRH Press Co., Ltd.,
in January 1989.

IRH PRESS
New York

Library of Congress Cataloging-in-Publication Data

ISBN 13: 978-1-942125-09-9
ISBN 10: 1-942125-09-7

Printed in China
First Edition
Second printing

Cover Design: Karla Baker
Cover image©Login/Shutterstock.com

CONTENTS

Preface   9

Chapter 1
The Secrets of Meditation

1 What Is Meditation?   12
The Essence of Meditation   13
The Purpose of Meditation   15
Achieving Inner Mastery   16

2 Inner Peace Meditation: Calming Your Thoughts   21
The Nature of Distracting Thoughts   23
Aligning Our Thoughts to Heaven   25
Choosing Inner Peace Over Distress   28
Creating Inner Peace at Will   30

3 Purposeful Meditation: Concentrating on an Aim   35

4 Reading Meditation: Training Your Mind to Focus   39

5 Opening the Mind to Inspiration   44

6 Meditation for Inner Conversation with Heaven: Connecting to Heaven   50

7 Finding Your Posture and Breathing Method   56
Hand Poses   57
Leg Poses   59
Breathing Methods   60

8 The Blessings of Meditation   63

9 The Secrets of Meditation   68

＊

Chapter 2
Meditations for Happiness

1 **Regaining Peace of Mind in a Conflictual Relationship**   74

2 **How to Calm the Mind**   81
Avoiding Contact With Others   81
Shifting Our Perspective to Solve Our Problems   83

3 **How to Find the Source of Confidence**   88
Accumulating Small Successes   88
Experiencing Our Divine Nature   90

4 **The Purpose of Meditation**   92

5 **Spontaneity Meditation:**
Finding Our True Self in the Freedom of Nature   96
＊Meditation to Become One with Nature   102

6 **Contentment Meditation:**
Discovering Our Blessings   106
＊Contemplation on Finding Contentment   109

7 **Relationship Harmony Meditation:**
Cultivating Understanding   115
＊Visualizing Relationship Harmony   121

8 **Self-Realization Meditation:**
Fulfilling God's Ideals   125
＊Three Keys to Successful Self-Realization Meditation   129

9 **Seeing Ourselves from the Minuscule Perspective and the Cosmic Perspective**   130

Chapter 3
Q&A on Meditation

1 How to Meditate When We Are Fatigued   134

2 How Visualization Works   141

3 Dealing with Interruptions during Meditation   140

4 To Whom Should We Pray?   157

5 Repelling Negative Spiritual Influences   163

6 Meditation for People with Dementia   170

7 On Reflection and Letting Go of the Past   174

Afterword   191

About the Author   193

About Happy Science   195

About IRH Press USA Inc.   203

Books by Ryuho Okawa   205

Preface

I wrote this book to share with the world the secrets that I have distilled from many years of meditative practice and unabated pursuit of the truths of meditation. I don't know of any other school of meditation that has developed its principles and practices, as I have, from the spiritual and miraculous impact that meditation has had on the teacher's own inner world.

I originally wrote or orally delivered each chapter with the members of Happy Science in mind, but I am certain that these secrets are universal and will be widely appealing to people of all walks of life. Chapter 1 combines two earlier works: an educational booklet about the essence of meditation that I originally wrote for members of Happy Science and a lecture I gave about this booklet in August 1988. Chapter 2 was originally my concluding lecture for a meditation seminar that featured my book *Meditations for Happiness*; it provides an overview of the meditations in that book. Finally, chapter 3 is a compilation of my answers to questions I received from the audience during these two events.

To my greatest pleasure, I present to you my philosophy of the true essence and art of meditation.

Ryuho Okawa
Founder and CEO
Happy Science Group

Chapter 1

The Secrets
of
Meditation

1

What Is Meditation?

Meditation is a richly deep and vast art, and today, it has grown into a widely practiced way of life. I am delighted to see the world's growing appreciation for this practice, but while a plethora of methods are offered, I could not find one that explains what meditation is really about.

Since so many people today have introduced this practice into their lives, I was inspired to share the knowledge and wisdom I have distilled from my own experience about the deeper truths of meditation. In this concise chapter, I have outlined an overview of my philosophy of the essence and secrets of meditation.

I hope that you won't let this chapter's simplicity deceive you. It is not meant to help you master meditation on your first try. Meditation is an elusive art that must be penetrated by practicing, not just by understanding the theory. I hope that the practices and principles that this chapter provides will help you gain a basic sense of what meditation is and how to practice it to benefit your daily life.

The Essence of Meditation

My philosophy of meditation may seem like a new perspective to modern people, but in truth, its wisdom is timeless. This same method was practiced 2,500 years ago by Shakyamuni Buddha, whose journey to inner awakening was based on the practice of meditation. Shakyamuni's meditation was an indispensable facet of his spiritual life and discipline, which he handed down to his disciples through his teachings. Men and women from age to age followed his method, which for thousands of years has continued to impact the lives of countless people.

How is my philosophy of meditation different from those you may already know about? A slew of methods have been offered by many people, but many misunderstandings remain about what meditation is really about. To begin with, meditation is not just about sitting with your eyes closed. Nor is it a technique for concentrating your mind on one thing. You may find many styles that teach you good posture and form and indulge you by creating a relaxing mood. But these methods, which strongly emphasize technique, associate meditation with a practice of form alone, rather than a practice of true substance. I have also found some methods, such as those taught by some Zen schools, that aim to make the mind a blank and encourage disbelief in God, Eternal Buddha, or the divine.

All of these concepts of meditation cannot be further from the truth. They lack the meaningful changes in inner awareness that are gleaned from true meditation.

Then what is the true essence of meditation? Clues can be found in the Japanese language; in Japan, "meditation" is eloquently written with two characters that mean "shut the eyes" and "think." This is an apt image, for meditation is a method of, first, shutting the eyes and removing worldly aspects from the mind, and second, thinking heavenly thoughts that establish an inner connection with heaven.

This chapter is, therefore, about meditation as a way to awaken your belief in the existence of the divinities of heaven and God, Eternal Buddha, or the Creator of the universe. For believing in a higher existence is the secret to achieving the inner transformation that meditation promises.

The Purpose of Meditation

Why do we need meditation? To find the answer, we must first consider our life from a spiritual perspective.

Heaven exists; this is an invariable Truth. We may have forgotten this truth, however, because we live in a physical world inside physical bodies that handicap our inherent awareness. This has led us to forget that heaven is our true home—that all of us were originally residents of a world of harmony and inner peace.

We human beings are thus inherently spiritual and heavenly. But when we were born into this world, we put on what strongly resembles a thick, clunky diving suit—the body. We use diving suits to protect us from the dangers underwater, such as cold temperatures, water pressure, darkness, hungry sharks, and turbulent deep sea currents. Like the depths of the sea, this world is a harsh environment for souls to live completely unprotected, so the physical body—

which can be likened to our full diving ensemble: the diving suit, air tank, flippers, and goggles—is indispensable to our survival in this world.

At the same time, this protective equipment naturally comes with repercussions—a numbing of our innate spiritual senses. Under these circumstances, we become so absorbed in surviving in these deep waters that memories of our spiritual nature fade from our wakeful consciousness. And the perfect inner freedom we once possessed becomes latent within the mind.

God is compassionate, however. He wishes for us to restore our inner freedom during this life. Therefore, he has imbued the human mind with the capacity to connect with heaven through a peaceful state of mind. Meditation is the method He has provided to calm the mind and align our inner state with that of heaven.

Achieving Inner Mastery

The mind is, in truth, the very essence of who we are. We can say with confidence that we are what we think. Yet the majority of us go through life without a conscious idea of what is happening in our mind and what it is capable of accomplishing. We may resemble a child who has a TV in front of her but does not know how to turn on the screen. We are waiting to be taught that a TV is used to watch TV programs and that to watch them, we need to turn it on and switch the channels to our desired show. Likewise, we need to understand what the mind does, learn how to awaken it, and practice switching the mind's channels.

The mind also resembles a remote control. Unless we know what a remote control is used for, we cannot tell that it has anything to do with the TV. We may never realize that it is a useful device that controls the TV, and in that case, we would never be able to put the remote to use.

The same holds true with our relationship with the mind. When we discover the mind's ability to transmit and display thought energies, we can start to use the mind for its true purpose. The mind possesses a sophisticated mechanism that sends and receives thoughts, much like a radio antenna that transmits radio frequencies.

The secret to turning on this power of the mind is to fine-tune the energy that it emanates by practic-

17

ing meditation. To continue the device comparison, the mind creates energies of varying frequencies throughout the day based on the types of thoughts we have. Some people refer to these frequencies as brain waves, and others call them the undulating waves of our thoughts and emotions.

Each of the thoughts we produce has its own characteristic energy. For example, distress is a type of thought that we create when we are facing many problems, and this energy is characterized by unsettling frequencies. Since frequencies attract each other, this unsettling energy may eventually attract even coarser energy to us—and thus, bigger problems.

Instead, we want the mind to have the opposite type of thoughts: thoughts of inner peace. Inner peace is a state of mind that is produced when our mind is calm for many days; our inner world has not been disturbed for a while, and the mind is still, ethereal, and filled with serenity.

If we take a moment to consider the thoughts that have swept through our own mind today, we can tell that our inner world is indeed producing many different frequencies. This is the reason why fine-tuning the mind is so essential. To control these frequencies, we need to make the effort to create the thought energy that we desire, such as inner peace.

The calm-breathing technique is a method that is very effective at creating calm thought energy. You would be surprised by how often we neglect this simple method. For example, this technique is especially useful when our anger has been ignited. It works even when the anger has blown into a state of complete rage, no matter how hopelessly we have lost control of ourselves and how terribly we are seething with resentment.

Technically, our anger may be a result of physiological causes, such as increased blood pressure or hormone imbalances. But calm breathing has such pacifying power over the emotions that in the end, these physical causes have little impact; the mind can be calmed quite quickly through a simple method of relaxed breathing.

"How is this possible? How does the way you control your breathing have any control over the mind?" you may wonder. First, breathing inward and outward in a rhythmic fashion has a relaxing effect on the muscles throughout the body, which in turn soothes our raging thoughts.

The mind in a state of anger is similar to a cup of dirt and water that is being shaken around. The soil particles keep swishing around and clouding the water. But when the cup is set down and allowed to be still, the soil particles begin to settle to the bottom, and a layer of clear water rises to the top.

The same principle is at work with the mind and body. When the mind has generated a storm of thoughts and emotions, the body is also tense and agitated—like the shaking cup—and the inner world is in the same chaotic state as the cloudy water. Practicing calm breathing is like setting the cup down—it relaxes the body, which then draws the mind into a state of calmness and stillness.

Gradually, we allow our mental dirt to separate from the pristine mind, and we allow the pristine layer alone to surface to consciousness. This beautiful layer of the mind represents the higher self within us—the true self—that emanates frequencies of tranquility that can then guide the mind to the wondrous, eternal worlds of heaven.

Meditation, in sum, is the practice of gaining mastery over our inner world to allow us to connect with heaven. This is the essence of meditation.

2

Inner Peace Meditation:
Calming Your Thoughts

Over the years, I have developed more than a dozen meditation programs to provide a variety of methods for gaining mastery over the mind and connecting to heaven. In fact, I created so many programs that most people have not been able to practice all of them. In the first few sections of this chapter, I present a basic framework and guidelines to help you derive the best benefits from your meditation practice. Broadly speaking, there are three different kinds of meditation.

The first kind of meditation is called *inner peace meditation.* This meditation is a way of fine-tuning the vibrations of the mind so that we may receive heaven's light and savor the bliss of inner peace. For many people, the mind is often in a scattered state.

A slew of thoughts, such as those about life's distresses, continuously sweep in and out of the mind throughout the day. So unless we make a deliberate effort to calm our mind, our inner world is going to remain in a state of disarray. We must train our mind to free itself of thoughts that are disharmonious to ourselves and the universe and aim to achieve a state in which tranquility alone pervades our whole being. We accomplish this by withdrawing the mind from negative thoughts and enriching it with musings about heaven instead, as if we were going on a vacation to the other world.

"Meditation to think nothing," a type of meditation practiced by men and women over the ages, does essentially the same thing. There is a common misconception that this form of meditation is about making your mind a blank. But the real aim is to find a complete state of relaxation by stopping distresses from emerging in the mind.

The aim of Zen practice, a very popular method these days, is also to create a state of inner peace. But the Zen method has some limitations as a style of meditation. Its strong emphasis on form and posture can prove helpful when someone is just starting out with meditation. But going through the motions alone does not lead to a truly meditative state. Reaching an authentic meditative state requires understanding why we really practice meditation: to free ourselves from negative thoughts, achieve divine awareness, and dwell in the bliss of inner peace.

The Nature of Distracting Thoughts

What are disharmonious thoughts, and how do we free the mind from their grasp? To understand the nature of disharmonious thoughts, I would like us to consider them in relation to the spiritual laws of the universe.

The universe is governed by spiritual laws that keep the world in a state of harmony. This restorative system returns the universe to a precise balance whenever it is set off-kilter. These laws may seem remote from individual life, but they are indeed at work in our daily lives to bring balance to thoughts that are misaligned with the Creator's order.

By virtue of being human, we have the freedom to think, ponder, and act as we desire. At the same time, however, every one of our actions either enriches or disrupts the harmony of the universe, and the invisible dynamics ensure that each action is always offset by a compensating reaction. A thought or deed that brings harm to anyone begets an equally forceful response from the universe. This is what results in a distracted mind, feelings of exasperation, emotions of anguish, and grief. This principle is an invariable truth of life that no one can ever change.

So whenever we struggle with a deep sense of unhappiness, it is important to consider what we might have done in the past to originate these feelings. Somewhere in the past, we may have sent out discordant energy, which is now returning to us as mental distress.

24

Of course, the universe does not only respond to negative energies; it also rewards thoughts and actions that advance the world's harmony, growth, and evolution. The universe's reward for benevolent acts is the opposite of disharmonious thoughts: the bliss of inner peace. We feel serene and are free from brooding, scattered thoughts and unsteady emotions. The mind is clear like a cloudless, sunlit sky, and inner peace flows through our being as effortlessly as a March stream. This may be a passive form of bliss, but it is the first essential stage of our journey to true happiness.

To find happiness when we are in a frenzied, distraught, and fretful state, we must train the mind to remove these distresses. For this reason, inner peace meditation is an essential practice for a happier way of life.

Aligning Our Thoughts to Heaven

Freedom from disruptive thoughts is essential for all methods of meditation and for self-reflection practices as well. For this reason, beginning meditators should start with inner peace meditation. Deeper meditative states remain inaccessible until you have mastered inner peace, and this requires a lot of effort. It may seem like a simple practice, but it is very difficult to achieve in reality. Beginners usually need to spend 70 percent of their meditations just focusing on stilling the mind.

I recommend that you begin inner peace meditation by relaxing your body. The mind and body have an intimate relationship: as you begin to release built up tension in your muscles, your mind will follow with greater ease. A good way to begin is by sitting with good posture and calming your breath. When your inner vibrations have relaxed, you will be ready for the next step.

The next step is to stop negative thoughts. To achieve this, we must concentrate not so much on banishing them from the mind, but rather on shifting the mind to positive thoughts. When I think of this step, I am reminded of an important lesson from the Buddhist monk, Nichiren. I wrote about his advice in my book entitled *The Spiritual Messages of Nichiren.* He explained, "To tame the mind, we must understand an important fact about its nature: the mind, as a matter of fact, is incapable of thinking two separate thoughts at the same time. This means that a negative thought cannot remain where a positive thought is present. What this principle of the mind shows is that when a negative thought gets stuck, like an iron nail on a wooden board, it can be more easily removed by hammering another nail—a positive thought—right over it. Do not fret about finding a way to pull it out. Instead, the negative thought can be hammered right out of the board by a positive thought."

God was indeed compassionate when he created us. He made us so that distress cannot remain where there is inner repose. He allowed just one thought to rule our inner kingdom at a given time. What this means is that we can remove worldly troubles from the mind by aligning our inner vibrations with a higher plane rather than by dwelling on negative thoughts.

The inner vibration or inner frequency of our worries is rarely attuned above the fourth dimension—in fact, our worries share the same frequencies as the dark realms of the other world. Therefore, there is no benefit to worrying about our distresses all the time.

When we attune our inner frequencies to those in heaven, it has the effect of keeping our worries, other people's distresses, our own distresses regarding others, and other people's thoughts about us from intruding into the mind. The frequencies become too different to be connected with each other.

Every day, many things happen that could cause us to have negative thoughts, whether they are situations that hurt our own feelings or something we did that hurt others. In every case, we have a choice: either to merely react to them or to choose to respond differently. If someone throws an insult at us or brings disappointing news, we have the choice to fret for the whole day, for a whole week or a whole year, or for our whole lives—or we can choose to let go of it immediately.

Choosing Inner Peace Over Distress

The more we practice inner peace meditation, the more skillful and swift we will be at resisting the influences of outer circumstances. We will be capable of entering a state of meditation at will. With this discipline, when life throws a stone into our inner lake, we will have the power to calm the ripples.

Someone else with no interest in inner mastery would probably feel these same ripples as if they were the stormy waves of a dark sea. This difference in the way we react comes from how we have trained our mind. For example, suppose that you are attending a meditation class and someone from the audience begins to argue with the speaker. Naturally, the tranquility that filled the class just a few minutes ago is now shattered.

Regardless of the outer circumstances, however, how each person's mind reacts to this situation is completely up to each individual. If you were in this situation, how long would it take you to regain a state of stillness, and when you did, for how long would you be able to preserve it? This is a chance to test how far your skills have advanced and a perfect opportunity to discover the fruits of your efforts.

Day-to-day experiences and encounters with other people, such as those in the example, are important challenges that discipline the mind to preserve inner calm. Inner peace meditation does not necessarily require set conditions, such as a secluded place or a Zen-like posture. In fact, it is supposed to be practiced within the circumstances of everyday life.

Life prepares a multitude of situations to teach us how to deal with the things people do, think, and say—to train us to make better decisions about how the events of life affect our inner world. What would you rather choose when the stone is tossed? Would you rather see the ripples rise into tumultuous waves or stop them and allow them to feather into tranquility? With effort, we can train the mind to react however we wish. With practice, you will become so skilled in this meditation that your mind will find its state of peace by the end of each day.

This way of life is closely related to a proverb that is well-loved in Japan: "Live each day as if it were your last." The mind is so versatile, with effort, we can train it to end our worries by bedtime. This is a secret to happiness that depends on the attitude we bring to each day. Each day is so precious. It would be a sad use of today if we were to fill it with the worries of yesterday. Likewise, tomorrow will bring problems of its own.

To cherish each day, we must realize that there is little worth in carrying one day's distresses into the next. To cherish tomorrow as much as we can, we must end today with peace of mind so we may begin the next morning with a fresh mind. This is what it means to live each day as if it were your last.

Creating Inner Peace at Will

This attitude eventually becomes second nature as we continue to master inner peace meditation: we begin to live not only each day, but also each hour, each minute, and each second as if they were our last. The ultimate aim of inner peace meditation is to train ourselves to stop the agitations of the mind the instant they arise, create inner peace at will, and maintain this state for as long as possible.

This ability is sometimes described as emitting

alpha waves. For example, Zen monks generate alpha waves during meditation. Beta waves are the opposite of that—the products of a distracted mind. Of course, it is not too difficult to maintain a peaceful mind when all you are doing is sitting and calming your breath. It is thanks to the challenges that day-to-day life offers that our mind has the chance to develop the skill of maintaining alpha waves under any circumstances.

Let's take an example. When someone says something hurtful, the most common reaction is to respond with anger and a retort. To create inner peace, we must instead develop the habit of immediately reflecting on ourselves and considering whether we might have been at fault.

Could something that we thought or did have provoked him to behave this way? In some situations, you will realize that the other person was simply reacting to your critical remark, put-down, or tormenting attitude, or to something else that you did or thought. If you discover that you were at fault, what you should do is clear: change your attitude right away and offer an apology. If the person is not with you, then you could apologize within your heart. This shift in your attitude—letting go of your hurt feelings—is as vital to your own well-being as it is to the other person's. Resentment is a very unhappy state of mind, and holding on to resentment for many days brings nothing of benefit.

On the other hand, if you cannot find a cause for the other person's behavior within yourself, then this is a situation that calls for forgiveness. Understandably, there are some occasions when we just can't shake off our hurt feelings, no matter how hard we try to forgive. In this case, look within and consider whether you are approaching this situation with enough love and determination to change your attitude. By love, I do not mean giving material gifts or acting with kindness. I mean the unconditional and nonjudgmental love that gives of itself with absolute goodwill.

We share this world with a multitude of people, each of whom is growing at a unique speed. So it is entirely possible that you understand something that others still do not. Therefore, patience is truly an important virtue as a member of our community. It is absurd to expect every person to follow your way of thinking. That would be like a teacher expecting all her students to immediately grasp everything she teaches exactly the way she teaches it. But the truth is that there are always some students who would learn better if they were given more time or a new approach.

I have authored many books, and have faced similar circumstances. While some of my readers understand 100 percent of my ideas, others understand 90 percent, 50 percent, or perhaps only 10 percent. But I don't allow this to frustrate me, because I see that these people have only just embarked on their journey to awakening. It would be narrow-minded for me to become exasperated only because someone doesn't share my perspective. If you make the conscious effort to bring this same kind of open-heartedness to all your encounters, your mind will eventually open itself to the spirit of forgiveness.

To cultivate a forgiving heart, we need enlightenment. That is, to truly be kind to others, we need a deep understanding of the human mind. When we understand the human mind deeply, it takes no effort to see why someone says something hurtful, why he is distressed about a problem, and why he behaves as he does. With this understanding, we cannot help but be kind.

But if we have not yet achieved this enlightenment and we are responding reactively, our inner world is

33

in the same state as his. His vibrations, since they are creating distress within us, are not coming from a place in heaven. And if our mind is reacting with the same disruptive energy, then our level of spiritual awareness is equal to his.

The choice is always open—you can always choose to bring your inner lake to stillness and allow your mind to shine like the full moon. Whatever the circumstances, you alone are responsible for your state of mind, because you have complete freedom to make the choice to change your attitude. Mastery of inner peace meditation is open to all who make the effort to live with a reflective mindset, to look at things from the standpoint of heaven, and to achieve a divine awareness of the self, others, and this world. This is the true purpose of meditation.

3

Purposeful Meditation:
Concentrating on an Aim

The second type of meditation is called *purposeful meditation*, which is any meditation that is practiced with a specific intent in mind. Reflective meditation, self-realization meditation, meditation for believing in your inner heavenly light, and meditation for remembering happy moments are just a few examples.

As their names imply, all these methods are practiced to achieve a clear purpose, which is accomplished by envisioning a goal upon the inner screen within the mind. As we visualize these goals unfolding, they become impressed upon the mind.

For example, the aim of reflective meditation is to clear the gloom of thoughts about the past that we have been holding onto too tightly and to come to terms with them. The thoughts that impede our inner peace usually come from feelings and perceptions that originated from past events. We must close our eyes, look back in time, and trace our memories. As we recall the events and thoughts of our past, they will come alive upon the inner lid of the eye or the inner screen of the mind, as if we were watching a home video. This helps us disengage ourselves from the images we see and study them from the standpoint of a detached observer.

To practice self-realization meditation, we envision a bright future for ourselves and imagine our potential coming to fruition. If, as we watch our lives unfold in the mind, our conscience remains confident that this is an ideal future for us, then we can be assured that this course of life will be worthy of our effort.

I cannot stress enough, however, that intense concentration aimed in the wrong direction can bring unwanted, even dangerous, situations upon ourselves. For this reason, it is vital to master inner peace meditation before beginning purposeful meditation. A calm and peaceful mind is essential to our ability to control the direction of our thoughts.

Many of the meditation methods offered these days teach students how to concentrate their thoughts on specific things. But these methods misunderstand the essence of meditation. Meditation and concentration are two different practices that require entirely different states of mind. We can concentrate our mind upon worldly thoughts, including thoughts that are disruptive to the harmony of the universe. In contrast, we can never achieve a meditative state by focusing on thoughts that are disharmonious to the world.

Whenever we focus the mind on something, we are making a strong inner connection with one of three possible worlds. Dark thoughts or intentions connect us with the world of hell. To be technical, they connect us with either hell or the astral realm, both of which are found in the fourth dimension of the other world.

The second world is a place called minor heaven. This is a world of sorcerers, hermits, and long-nosed wizards who use the power of concentration to create physical phenomena; their efforts characteristically lack spirituality and a sense of right and wrong. In their world, you will find, for example, people who like to use the power of the mind to bend spoons and forks.

I experimented with this ability myself once, and

I managed to bend two spoons and break three forks. But I decided not to continue this kind of practice because, during my concentration, I was visited by a *tengu* spirit, a type of long-nosed wizard, who came to help me develop this power. From this experiment, I quickly learned that concentrating on physical objects connected my inner world with spirits like these.

I wasn't interested at all in having those kinds of power. And I felt that something was not right about this manner of concentrating my willpower. What's more, I noticed that the intensity of concentration in this practice is so strong that the mind becomes connected instantly, within one or two seconds. I realized that this practice would give me a lot of power, but that it was clearly a dangerous kind.

I believe that everyone should aim to connect with heaven, the third type of world, when they are practicing concentration.

4

Reading Meditation:
Training Your Mind to Focus

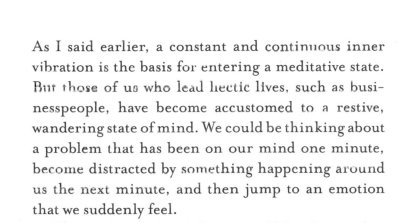

As I said earlier, a constant and continuous inner vibration is the basis for entering a meditative state. But those of us who lead hectic lives, such as businesspeople, have become accustomed to a restive, wandering state of mind. We could be thinking about a problem that has been on our mind one minute, become distracted by something happening around us the next minute, and then jump to an emotion that we suddenly feel.

Those of us with a diffuse mind like this need to regain the ability to shut out worldly thoughts that interrupt our concentration and impede us from diving into a deep meditative state. This should be your first step in meditation if you have an active, busy life.

By now, you may be thinking, "If only I could manage to find a week's worth of time—then, I would go somewhere quietly tucked away, like a mountainside retreat, to meditate. Then I wouldn't have to worry about distractions or interruptions, and I would make a lot of progress." But much to our dismay, life is often far too demanding of our time for a trip away and too hectic to provide proper surroundings for meditation at home. This is the challenge of a busy modern life.

If this situation sounds familiar to you, there is no need to be disheartened by your circumstances, because there are achievable steps that you can take even under these circumstances. No matter what situation we face, the mind can be disciplined to work for us, just as a magnetic compass always points in one direction no matter how we move it. Similarly, we can learn to direct the mind to a single vibration and focus on it for as long as possible.

What I would like to recommend is a method called reading meditation. The aim is for your inner world to be absorbed in the book for a long span of time without letting yourself be distracted by something else.

How do we practice reading meditation? It is

important to choose reading material that is of high spiritual caliber but that does not require a lot of intellectual work. For example, many magazines, tabloids, and philosophical books would be poor choices. If you are interested in my teachings, I highly recommend the books that I have published. They are very effective for reading meditation.

Next, you should set a pace and length of time to spend reading that will work for you so that you can completely immerse your mind in your book for a while. You could highlight sentences as you go if this works for you. Your target may be to read a third of the way or halfway through your book each time you practice. You could also measure your goal by time, if you would like; I would recommend spending at least one to two hours each time. If, at first, one hour feels too long to focus your mind, you can begin with thirty minutes or even fifteen minutes. Then you can gradually increase this span to one hour, then two hours, and then three hours. When you come this far, you will have the ability to quickly restore your mind to a calm state.

If you work, I recommend practicing reading meditation during your commute. Your commute time is an ideal environment, especially if you use public transportation in a big city. A packed subway or bus during rush hour is a perfect storm of distractions that will really challenge your mind's ability to focus: there are people, voices, other noises, and newspapers that your mind could be tempted to wander off to. And this is a time of day when your thoughts are prone to trailing off to the project you are currently working on or the fight you just had with your spouse at breakfast.

As you read, you will notice that your attention keeps wandering off, whether it is to boredom by the fifth page, to the pot on the stove by the fifteenth page, to a TV show by the thirtieth page, or to an urge to give up by the twentieth page. Each time you notice that your mind has scattered away, simply return your attention to the words. This is challenging work, which makes this a discipline with tremendous rewards.

If you can discipline yourself to keep removing distractions from your mind under these circumstances for, say, a whole hour, and give the book your undivided attention, your concentration skills will make remarkable progress. You will not only cultivate the ability to focus your mind, but also train your mind to attune its inner vibrations to thoughts of high spiritual value.

There may be circumstances in which you encounter a physical limitation to reading. For example, if you live in a very crowded city with trains crammed with people wall to wall, it may be difficult to find enough space to open your book. In a circumstance like this, you might choose to forgo reading and instead spend your time contemplating a topic. For example, you could try meditating on a topic about the principle of hope—that because your mind is aligned with God, you will receive His guidance. Or, you could contemplate about how to develop intuitive intelligence—intelligence that cultivates knowledge and logical thinking into spiritual awareness. You could also choose a key theme from my teachings—for example, "love that gives."

Ultimately, reading meditation will help you cultivate the concentration skills that are essential for mastering inner peace meditation. In addition, it will prepare you to practice purposeful meditation with great ease. This skill will also be vital when you begin to explore the other methods of meditation I offer.

43

5

Opening the Mind to Inspiration

When we master reading meditation and inner peace meditation, we will be ready to move on to purposeful meditation.

I would like to consider an important question that people frequently ask about purposeful meditation: to practice purposeful meditation, do we need to concentrate our willpower and actively form the images through a lot of concerted effort? The answer is yes and no.

As I explained earlier, the first step of meditation is to concentrate the mind as though we are narrowing the focus on a camera lens in order to rid our minds of disruptive this-worldly thoughts. Concentrating the mind on one thing is essential, as long as we do not direct our thoughts toward the wrong inner vibration.

44

However, this alone does not allow us to find the meditative state we want. When the mind establishes a steady focus on one inner vibration and is capable of maintaining this state for a long span of time, we must move on to the next step of opening up the mind to receive inspirations while keeping our focus intact.

We will not make this transition if we try to create our own images upon the inner screen, because that would represent attachment to something we wish to see. This wish to see inhibits our inner world from opening and relaxing. The images must be allowed to appear of their own volition, and we must accept whatever unfolds with an attitude of full acceptance. When we keep thinking about what we wish to have and what we want to achieve, our state of mind resembles a person who is hunching over or a person wearing a raincoat. Just as a raincoat is a layer of clothing that repels all the raindrops and keeps them from soaking into our bodies, our wishes form a layer of thought that deflects the precious guidance of divine spirits from reaching our heart.

Instead, we must accept the divine spirits' inspirations without hesitation and with an open mind. Ultimately, purposeful meditation is not about creating visions using our own volition. Rather, the ultimate purpose is to open the inner world so that we are allowing authentic images from heaven to emerge from deep within the mind.

For example, reflective meditation is a way of entering a meditative state through the practice of self-reflection. Shakyamuni Buddha espoused this method as the basis of his meditations.

During the practice of reflective meditation, we do look back at our life and recall events of the past, but these images should eventually unfold vividly within the mind without any strong intention on our part.

For example, if we remember a mistake that we made as a child, the scene that we are shown on the inner screen should not be a scene that we are trying to see, but a scene that has surfaced from our depths. We are not trying to see it, but allowing it to appear. Though the difference may seem subtle, it is vital.

There is a point, during reflective meditation, when our state of mind transitions into an authentic meditative state. This transition happens when we advance from an effortful, intentional state to a passive, receptive state. This point of transition is the key to a truly meditative state.

Purposeful meditation, therefore, does not demand intense, effortful concentration or intentional visualization. Instead, it requires a receptive, open state of mind, which is achieved by maintaining a calm and focused inner vibration. In addition, we must wholeheartedly accept whatever kinds of visions emerge upon the inner screen for what they are.

This ability to bring your inner world to an open state is a prerequisite for advancing to the third kind of meditation that achieves inner contact with heaven. This makes sense, because the images that appear to us during this meditation are sent to us from heaven, which is the opposite of working to create them on our own.

It is difficult to comprehend how we are able to receive support from divine spirits in heaven and what it means to create a state of inner receptiveness when we haven't experienced these things. It may be difficult to understand, but it is definite that someone who has reached this state of mind will make that inner connection with divine spirits and will begin receiving their valuable guidance.

It may seem to us as though we are practicing reflective meditation all on our own, but in truth, the hints that arise are always blessings from someone residing in heaven. We receive inspiration from above to help us notice important things, which then unfold as the mental images that we see. We cannot perfect our practice of meditation without making our mind receptive to these inspirations.

The same principle holds true for self-realization meditation. First, we need to focus our thoughts on realizing a bright future. But then, in the next step, we must open the mind and wait calmly for images to arise of their own accord.

A myriad of books and speakers on self-realization talk a lot about using your willpower to actualize your goals. These methods are fundamentally different from self-realization meditation. Their methods can be practiced even if worldly thoughts and energies are in constant command of our inner world. According to them, by the principle of attraction, we are capable of realizing a wish such as to buy a bigger house by thinking continuously, daily, about how much we want to achieve that wish.

These writers and speakers espouse the use of focused willpower to achieve worldly purposes—to actualize material things. This may be an effective method of accomplishing an aim, but it is not a method of meditation or an ideal approach to life.

Instead of connecting us to heaven, this practice connects our inner world to the likes of sorcerers, hermits, and wizards.

My meditation for self-realization allows us to envision images of the future that are aligned with the wishes of the guardian and guiding spirits, and this should be the true goal of our meditation.

6

Meditation for Inner Conversation with Heaven:
Connecting to Heaven

The third kind of meditation is called the *meditation for inner conversation with heaven*. In this stage, our foothold is no longer based in this world as it was during purposeful meditation. Now, the mind becomes directly connected to heaven and we are able to have inner exchanges with our guardian and guiding spirits—spiritual beings who watch over and support us from heaven throughout our life.

In essence, we become one with heaven, and we are cultivating our spirituality so that we can develop the heart of a heavenly person. The ultimate aim of this stage of meditation is to arrive at the very culmination of this art: a truly meditative state of mind and a true grasp of what it means to practice meditation.

Before I go on further, I would like to review the steps we have discussed so far. First, we direct our inner world to thoughts of high spirituality and maintain this state of mind for as long as possible. This helps us enter deeply into a meditative state and enables us to shut out worries, problems, and other this-worldly thoughts that might disturb our inner peace.

Once we reach this state, the next step is to practice purposeful meditation. This is a practical form of meditation in which we set goals that assist our spiritual discipline and mental training. There is an endless variety of purposeful meditations—there are as many kinds as there are goals. However, the final aim of meditation lies beyond these purposes, so we must gradually abandon them when we reach the third step.

As our state of mind becomes more intensely focused in the second stage, our inner world will eventually transition to a state of complete receptiveness to the inspirations of heaven. The purposeful intent that we initially cultivated opens up to allow in the guidance of divine spirits.

This is the point at which we reach the third stage and our communication with heaven begins on a fuller scale than before. Gradually, we notice that the perceptions of our five senses, including hearing and sight, have diminished, even though we are still within our physical bodies, and that the spiritual aspect of these senses has become heightened. This occurs because we begin to perceive our surroundings through the spiritual body rather than the physical body.

The effort you devote to the earlier stages will allow you to gradually enter a state of mind that may eventually lead further, to out-of-body experiences. The ability to think continuously about topics of high spiritual value, which you developed through reading meditation is an essential condition that establishes this communication.

These out-of-body experiences require a highly advanced state of mind. This state of mind deserves in-depth discussion in another book, but I will provide a brief overview here. There are many degrees of this experience, but those who have advanced very far can catch glimpses of heaven and feel the presence of divine spirits within themselves. For example, Shakyamuni Buddha had this experience many times during his meditations, and his soul frequently traveled back and forth to heaven. Divine spirits were always with him, as well, often speaking to him, and he sometimes felt God's light flooding his whole being.

This type of meditation that allows us to have conversations with heaven really does exist. It may be difficult for the majority of us to reach the state that Shakyamuni Buddha achieved, but a very common type of connection that many beginning meditators experience is a warm sensation within the heart in the middle of meditation. Many people who come to hear me speak have had this same experience happen to them as they sat in the audience.

There are other ways that we may experience this warmth, too. Some of us may feel the warmth flow into us from above the head. Or we may feel a rush of warm circulation run through our body, a flush of warmth fill our chest, or a sudden flooding of warmth the moment we encounter words of Truth.

All of these are signs of a connection with our guardian spirit. Our guardian spirit may be sending us light from heaven to help us realize something important about our life, or the guardian spirit may be having a moment of spiritual awareness. These are experiences of God's light that help awaken our soul to the Truths.

53

Everyone is capable of experiencing such moments. Although it may take a number of years to reach this point, the effort you put into learning about the Truths, by attending talks and seminars for instance, will eventually bear fruit. You will gradually see more of these moments come to you.

I hope that you will also experience this inner bliss someday. This is certainly the kind of experience that will bring you to a higher spiritual awareness and a deeper sense of meditation and spirituality. Your spirituality will heighten to the degree that you will know precisely how to create inner peace and to read your own state of mind like an open book. It will become easier to recognize when your mind has fallen into a state of suffering and is going through a lot of inner turmoil. And as soon as you restore peace to the inner world, for example through self-reflection, you will immediately feel your mind filled with light.

I hope you understand now that inner dialogue with heaven is within your grasp and that your comprehension of the essence of meditation will change forever when you experience this for yourself. It is so profound that it will transform the way you understand what it means to be in a receptive state of mind. Though this is a difficult stage of meditation to achieve, I believe that, with effort, many people can cultivate this inner state and that heavenly experiences are within reach for everyone.

7

Finding Your
Posture and Breathing Method

When you think of meditation postures, what comes to your mind? Is it the kneeling posture of Zen monks, the elaborate cross-legged positions of yogis, the upward and downward hand placements—mudras —of Buddhist statues, or perhaps the prayer pose?

This section describes postures and breathing techniques for meditation. But these are merely recommendations to help you begin your practice as comfortably as possible. There are no hard-and-fast rules that have to be followed and there are many postures that work.

If you were to ask me how I meditate, I would have to confess that I've had no trouble meditating while eating dinner or even during a nap. If someone asked me to, I think I could even meditate while doing a handstand. Experience has taught me that in the end, posture and technique have little to do with achieving a meditative state of mind.

Having said that, I still recommend following some basic guidelines for posture and breathing to help you meditate comfortably.

Hand Poses

Many different hand positions have been used throughout the ages, and each has its advantages. I recommend three different hand positions for inner peace meditation, purposeful meditation, and med

itation for inner conversation with heaven.

When you practice inner peace meditation, I recommend laying your hands on your knees with the palms open and faced up. This posture promotes a sense of liberation and helps the body and the mind relax, which assists in banishing worldly thoughts that disrupt inner peace.

The best hand position for purposeful meditation is laying the hands on the knees with the palms faced down, which represents concentration. This posture encourages active thinking and strengthens the ability to concentrate in a dynamic way. It is especially well suited for long periods of meditation.

The prayer pose is best suited for meditation for inner conversation with heaven and for out-of-body meditation. This is the most commonly used pose for these types of meditations and is formed by holding the palms of the hands together in a prayer gesture in front of the chest.

The prayer pose is the best posture for meditations and prayers that aim to connect us to divine spirits. The hands are one of the spiritual centers of the body and have the ability to concentrate and transmit God's light. For example, you may have heard stories of healing achieved by laying the hands on the body. Pointing our hands in a particular direction helps us concentrate our inner vibration in that direction. If our hands point upward, our inner thoughts are directed to heaven. Our fingers become antennas that send forth our spiritual energy, and this allows us to reach the divine spirits. This principle resembles placing a phone call to heaven. Just as people pick up the phone when they receive a call, when our energy reaches heaven during our meditation, a divine spirit with similar inner vibrations picks up "the other end of the line."

The prayer pose also represents a middle-way state of mind that is balanced between two extremes. For example, when your mind is agitated, taking the prayer pose should subdue your frustrations, and you should feel much calmer and balanced.

The next time you become upset about something, try this experiment: hold your hands in front of your chest in the prayer pose, and see whether you are able to stay upset. It should be very difficult to continue generating angry energy. Soon, you will feel your anger begin to subdue. Prayer pose is indeed a very effective way to restore inner peace to the mind.

59

Leg Poses

Many different leg postures, such as the lotus pose and kneeling, have also been practiced throughout the ages, but these are not essential. The most important point is to find a posture that feels comfortable to you and that will assist your concentration. Since meditation can go on for a while, I recommend finding a relaxed posture that you can maintain for a long time without it disrupting your focus. And if possible, I recommend sitting with the head and neck in a straight line, not in a rigid way, but in an easy, upright posture, to ward off sleepiness.

Personally, I don't use the kneeling position for a very simple reason: my legs fall asleep quite quickly. And I don't use the full lotus pose, either, also for a simple reason: I have difficulty contorting my legs into this position—perhaps because my legs are too long or too short, I can't tell which—but regardless, it just doesn't feel comfortable to me, so I'm certain others may have the same trouble with it.

Breathing Methods

The next step is to calm your breathing. Begin your breathing exercise by inhaling deeply through the nose and chest, allowing the breath to reach the stomach. Then, exhale gently and slowly through the mouth. As you alternate between inhaling and exhaling, the rhythm of your breaths will help calm your mind.

There are many other breathing techniques. For example, one of my meditations uses the opposite technique: inhaling through the mouth and exhaling through the nose. I have heard of other methods in which the meditator breathes in and out through just the nose or just the mouth. Which one we choose is a matter of preference that depends on our physical disposition. Those who have no problem breathing through the nose may benefit from using that method, while those who can breathe only shallowly through the nose should breathe through their mouth.

I have experimented with different methods myself. When I tried breathing in and out only through the nose, my breath became so shallow that after a couple of minutes, my face began to turn red. So I've learned that using my mouth suits my physiology much better. But those who are slim and have no trouble breathing deeply through the nose may find that breathing only through the nose works for them.

The difference between breathing through the nose and breathing through the mouth is basically the amount of oxygen each method gets us. Inhaling through the mouth gives us more oxygen quickly. It works so quickly that it will help you calm your mind instantly, which may be why this method is more popular.

For example, when you are on the verge of losing

your temper, I recommend inhaling through the mouth and exhaling slowly through the nose. If you repeat this two or three times, your temper will calm down. It will take you much longer—about five minutes—to soothe your temper by inhaling through the nose. So I recommend choosing the method that suits you and your current state of mind.

Shakyamuni Buddha's order preferred the method of inhaling through the nose and exhaling through the mouth, because inhaling and exhaling through only the nose or only the mouth is the way that we normally breathe. Using a method that we are not used to helps us be more conscious of our breathing. This method also makes it easier to bring our breath and awareness down to our stomach.

The key is to find the breathing method that is most comfortable to you and that works best to calm your mind and body. Through persistent practice, these breathing techniques will help you restore inner peace to your mind. And those who have achieved a certain degree of spiritual awareness will experience the warmth of divine light just by calming their breathing.

8

The Blessings of Meditation

Meditation brings many blessings to our inner world and happiness. There are three main benefits that we gain from making meditation a part of our life.

First, meditation gives our inner world valuable relief from the troubles and anxieties that beset us night and day. Many people's minds are so plagued by problems that they hardly have a moment of peace to savor. For many people, the greatest impediments to happiness are this-worldly issues and needless worries about the future that take hold of the mind.

Practicing meditation helps us shift away from our inner turmoil, even if only for a little while, to bring us a passive, calm sense of happiness. Persistent practice trains our inner world to let go of these unsettling energies and allow them to drift away, like the freely flowing stream of a spring meadow. This vital benefit of meditation supports the health and happiness of the mind.

Second, meditation allows us to experience an ethereal state of happiness that is very real and authentic. In these small moments of spiritual enlightenment, we sense the presence of divine spirits beside us, feel the shower of celestial light upon us, and catch glimpses of the blissful worlds of heaven; these are the moments that teach us what it really means to be happy. Nothing in this physical world can ever compare to this heavenly bliss. With continued practice of meditation, a feeling of carefree joy and complete happiness will pervade you, and you will experience moments of this simple bliss again and again.

I have experienced this myself and could speak about it at length. When we experience the presence of divine light and divine spirits beside us and realize how real they are, a flood of emotion overcomes us. I don't know anyone who could cease the stream of hot tears upon their cheeks when they discover that their guardian spirit has been beside them all these years, watching over and guiding them, even through years of careless living.

Discovering such Truths brings joyous tears beyond description. Our hearts become flooded with gratitude for those who have always supported us despite our never noticing their existence, for our life ahead, and for the possibilities of the future. No one could hold back the surge of warmth that overtake our inner world in such moments of rapture. It is a happiness that doesn't compare to anything we have felt before. Those who practice meditation will experience this someday, and it is my sincere hope that as many people as possible will have the opportunity to savor this joy.

There is an even higher state of happiness, experienced by saints such as Shakyamuni Buddha, which is the fuller bliss that great enlightenment brings. This is an exalted joy utterly beyond words that is only achieved through spiritual awakening. Those who achieve this level of enlightenment discover the true meaning of human existence, become aware that they are part of a vast universe, and awaken to their unique purpose in life.

These awakenings inspire tremendous joy and rouse a burning passion of delight. Once we experience this, everything of any worth in this physical world pales in comparison to the bliss we feel. The value you used to feel for anything now feels hollow and vain, and your only desire now is to abandon all that is in your possession. This state of spiritual delight is difficult for most to reach, but it is a goal to which all seekers should aspire. I hope that you now understand the immense worth of achieving such a level of enlightenment while still in the flesh.

Enlightenment is relative to each person, and I believe that we can consider great enlightenment according to our own level of spirituality—the original spiritual awareness we possessed in heaven. It is a huge endeavor to cultivate this awareness in the circumstances of this physical world. If we can achieve the ability to sense, think, understand, and act the way we would have in our purely spiritual form, such a state of mind will surely bring great joy to our life. It is my sincerest hope that many people will be able to experience such happiness in this life, and for this purpose, Happy Science offers many centers around the world.

Finally, meditation enables us to take control of our destiny and achieve mastery over life. There are times in life when we lose hold of the steering wheel and are swept off course by the worldly currents of destiny. Sometimes we hardly realize that this has happened and end up drifting downward unknowingly. But we eventually realize that we must regain our control. As I wrote in one of my prayers, "The

Dharma of the Right Mind," we have the inherent capacity to take control of the boat of our life.

Meditation helps us restore inner peace and then enables us to grasp the essence of who we are and the essence of God and the divinities—including understanding how heaven perceives us. Seeing our life from heaven's perspective helps us understand what we must do to take command of our life. By this, I mean that introspection helps us discover what kind of river we are riding, what currents are beneath our boat, what type of boat we are steering, and what we must ultimately do to take command. We begin to understand our mind and actions and become aware of where we stand in this world and how we have been steering ourselves so far. So when we realize that we have deviated from our path, meditation helps us determine how to steer our life back to its proper path.

67

Meditation helps us cultivate a perspective on life based on heaven's point of view, and this is the very key to mastering life. This is such an effective practice that the distance traveled by those who practice it and those who neglect it will be vastly different. This is the essence and secret of meditation.

9

The Secrets of Meditation

To conclude this chapter, I would like to sum up the secrets that will lead your meditations to higher levels of spirituality.

The raison d'etre of meditation is to cultivate a relationship with heaven. The first secret of meditation is to believe wholeheartedly in God, Eternal Buddha, or the divine. When we do not believe in the power of the source of meditation, we deprive it of its impact upon us. When we practice with an attitude of disbelief, we are merely concentrating on material and worldly thoughts, which is the reverse of the peaceful and receptive state that allows our inner world to receive divine light and guidance. As I explained earlier, some styles of meditation aim to deny divine existence. Those who espouse these methods do so only because they are unaware of the truth, and their practices lack spiritual experience and inner wisdom. I believe that those who teach and practice meditation have a responsibility to pursue the truth for themselves.

The second secret of meditation is to subdue any self-serving aims that may be motivating our practice. Purely self-concerned objectives hardly deserve the light and guidance of heaven, for such desires foster vile energy. Instead, our desire for self-improvement must come from a higher purpose, such as to manifest God's Will in this world. Like a servant of God or a soldier of heaven, we seek heaven's strength for the sake of achieving an exalted purpose and request divine guidance in manifesting our true inner potential to fulfill these aims.

Some people think of meditation as a way to fulfill a self-gratifying purpose, such as cultivating psychic energy or occult, paranormal powers. But this is different from a selfless mindset, and it carries great risks. Intentions like these may eventually connect our inner world to darker worlds of the wrong, hellish energy.

Last but not least, the third secret of meditation is to frequently review our life and the state of this world from the standpoint of heaven. We aspire to align our understanding of where we stand in life with heaven's point-of-view.

Before I conclude, I would like to explain these three secrets from a slightly different angle, based on their association with the worlds in heaven.

The first secret, having faith, is an attitude that is shared by heaven's angels and arhats, who live in the World of Light (also called the sixth dimension). The souls of this world have a deep appreciation for the spiritual Truths created by God, Eternal Buddha, or the Creator, and they devote themselves to enriching their spiritual knowledge and faith.

The second secret, meditating to fulfill an unselfish purpose, is a mindset that is shared by the angels and bodhisattvas of the World of Bodhisattvas (also called the seventh dimension). This means that if your way of life is based on love for others, then your thoughts will reach this part of heaven during meditation. Described in a more proactive way, if you are devoted to compassion for others and altruistic intentions, you will receive the divine guidance of the spirits of the seventh dimension.

Finally, when you have perfected the third secret —a deep awareness of your life and the state of this world from heaven's point-of-view—your state of mind will be shared by the World of Tathagatas (also called the eighth dimension). The divine spirits of this world, the tathagatas, are so spiritually aware that they have become embodiments of the Truths, the universal Laws of God. They have a deep understanding of the Laws and God's heart, and they make decisions based on God's true desires. In every situation they encounter through life, their leadership is nearly flawless: they know where God's Will stands and how He would perceive the situation, and they handle problems as God would manage them.

I have described the three secrets of meditation in relation to the worlds of heaven so that you understand the places that we are capable of reaching through meditation. Progression through these worlds is the ultimate aim of meditation.

Life's problems and suffering ultimately arise from forgetting to live with heaven's perspective as our own. However, even if we sometimes drift into worldly thoughts and emotions, meditation is an extraordinary, blissful experience that cultivates our capacity to understand our own state of mind as those in heaven do, even while we live in this world. This is the miracle of meditation. Persistent practice will lead you to achieve great things in life and will open the way to a bright future.

Chapter 2

Meditations
for
Happiness

1

Regaining Peace of Mind in a Conflictual Relationship

When we interact with other people, we may sometimes notice their faults and shortcomings, and we may be surprised to find ourselves feeling proud and smug as a result. But we need to remind ourselves that noticing other people's shortcomings proves nothing other than the fact that we are not completely insensitive. Noticing other people's flaws by no means proves our own greatness.

What proves our greatness is the ability to see through these things to the light of Truth that brightens up their life, while at the same time remaining mindful of how they look, how they live, and their state of mind. This ability enables us to understand the true meaning of life, to progress in our spiritual discipline, and to walk the path to enlightenment.

I myself am still learning in this regard. I am probably very good at spotting other people's flaws when I try, but the reason my audiences feel at ease when I give talks is that they are certain that I will not start condemning them. If I were the type of person who makes a habit of pointing out people's flaws as soon as they sit down in front of me, I'm sure the front-row seats would be completely empty. The whole audience would probably sit in the back if they thought I would be pointing out every single mistake they've ever made—for example, how they got into a fight with someone over such and such an issue.

But I would never point out what's wrong with the people in my audiences, and because they know that, they can sit in front of me with peace of mind. This sense of trust is extremely important in building harmonious relationships. We inevitably feel nervous around people who constantly point out our mistakes and faults.

But what do we do when we can't help but notice other people's shortcomings? How do we stay lenient and focus on the good in them instead? What is the key to acquiring such an attitude? It is getting to know others. It is appreciating different people's values. It is understanding how the human mind works and how people think. This is what is meant by the saying, "To know all is to forgive all." It is often because we don't know others that we misunderstand one another, and it is this misunderstanding that can bring about unhappiness.

In my book *The Laws of the Sun*, I said that evil does not exist in and of itself. Evil is a distortion caused by conflict between souls, which have been granted total freedom to create what they wish. This is the origin of evil. Evil comes into existence only when we come into contact with another person. This is very true.

There is something wonderful about each and every one of the people we see around us. But the wonderful parts of each person can come into conflict as differences of opinion when we try to work, live, and do things together. Our conflicting perspectives can evolve into something even more wonderful when we are able to resolve them through constructive discussion. It is when we insist that we are absolutely right and refuse to compromise or come to terms with others that evil arises. Self-righteousness and self-assertiveness give rise to evil.

I've offered advice and counsel on many issues in life. I have received a lot of letters from my readers asking for advice on how to solve their problems. When

I read their letters, I see that more than 90 percent of them are laying the blame not on themselves, but on others or on their circumstances. It is very difficult to offer sound advice to these people, because as long as they attribute their unhappiness to their family members, parents or siblings, or their circumstances, they will not be able to change themselves, no matter what kind of advice I give them. I cannot change the fact that they were born into a certain family or who their parents are. I cannot change the fact that they were born with their brothers or sisters. And I cannot change the fact that they had an underprivileged upbringing.

The only thing they can change is how they feel about their circumstances and experiences, how they interpret them, and how they will make use of them as they move forward in life. We cannot change the basic facts of our circumstances. Even prayers won't instantaneously transform reality into your ideal world. My advice to these readers will be fruitless as long as they continue to look for solutions outside themselves. They won't be able to change their circumstances until they stop placing the blame for their problems on their friends, teachers, and coworkers and the other people around them.

Every day, our mind reacts to the various events

that happen around us, and we experience all kinds of feelings. Whatever circumstances we find ourselves in, the first step is to control our own mind by asking ourselves whether it is right to feel the way we do. Before you interpret and react to something that someone has said to you, ask yourself whether you are taking their words in the right way.

We can interpret others' words in many different ways. Perhaps you are misunderstanding their intended meaning. You may be taking their kind words as empty flattery or suspecting them of concealing an ulterior motive designed to take advantage of you later, when all they are really trying to do is offer you encouragement.

We need to examine our perceptions and reactions objectively and consider whether they were really accurate. This introspection is essential to maintaining peace of mind. When we feel that others have said something wrong, there is always a chance that we have taken their words the wrong way.

Suppose that someone has said something unpleasant to you, and you feel that, no matter how you take it, their words were offensive. But perhaps you could simply choose not to let it bother you. Perhaps you are taking it very seriously and think that their words are violating your dignity, and so you choose to fight back. Such a situation could well turn into a battle of words that further escalates the conflict, strains the relationship, and snowballs into a major problem. But if you quietly and detachedly search for the cause of the conflict, very often you will find that the cause is related to your own emotional reactions and your ability to process those feelings.

I am keenly sensitive to other people's feelings. I have the ability to sense their emotions, but fortunately, I am very gifted at not feeling them, too. This ability makes me impervious to criticism and slander. I can let criticism pass right through me, because I have learned to see things from diverse perspectives.

For example, let's say that I arrived twenty minutes late to the venue of my lecture, and I had to push back my lunchtime. Suppose that I made small talk at the beginning of my talk and did not go right into the main topic, and Mr. A thought that I did that because I needed time to digest my meal. If he told me what he thought, I wouldn't take offence. Mr. A might actually have guessed right. I would simply think, "He has a point—I do sometimes have days when I don't feel like going straight into the main topic." If I took his words seriously and made a big deal out of it, it could easily turn into a big problem.

This ability to let things pass through you is essential to your meditation practice, because the first key to a successful meditation practice is to maintain a peaceful and undisturbed mind. Before we meditate, we must first be able to minimize the turbulence that disturbs our mind. To do that, we need to train ourselves to take lightly what other people say and do to us or even let them go completely—so that our mind can remain unshakable and calm.

2

How to Calm the Mind

Avoiding Contact With Others

There are two basic ways to achieve a calm, undisturbed mind. The first is to avoid contact with other people. Since ancient times, many religious practitioners have tried to create solitude. They would sequester themselves in a cave or a remote village to meditate. These are still effective ways to achieve a calm mind. Retreating to a quiet place and avoiding contact with others makes it easier to maintain peace of mind because solitude makes us less susceptible to other people's mental energies.

It is not that difficult to harmonize our mind when we are alone. For this reason, spending time alone is essential for beginning meditators. But most of us live busy lives, and solitude is not always an option in today's hectic society. The more capable and the more recognized in society we become, the more complex our life becomes. We live in an era that requires us to multitask. Those who have become successful and are in a position to guide and lead others are becoming increasingly busy. Some of them even sacrifice their private life for work.

Meditation is meant to be a means for great souls to increase their power twofold, threefold, or even five-, ten-, or a hundredfold. This means that meditation is all the more important for busy people whose social standing is high, because we very much need these people to cultivate and unleash their true potential. But what should they do if they simply cannot take the time to be alone?

When our circumstances do not allow us to avoid contact with others or escape from outside influences, there is only one way to maintain serenity within. It is to control how we feel about and react to outside influences. There is nothing we can do about what people think and do. All we can do is choose how to interpret their words and actions and learn what we can from them. This is the spiritual discipline we can practice to maintain a harmonious mind in the course of our busy, day-to-day lives.

Shifting Our Perspective to Solve Our Problems

One way to control how we feel about and react to what happens outside us is to train ourselves to shift our perspective as fast as we can. This is the first step we can take. Many of us don't even think about changing our perspective. This is because we don't learn how to control the mind at school; we usually don't have anyone who can guide us or point out when our mind is disturbed. But the truth is that each of us is given complete control over the kingdom of the mind.

We need to take the time to introspect and review everything that we think and feel. If you get eight hours of sleep, take some time each day to examine what you thought and felt in the sixteen hours when you are awake. Most often, we find that our mind was filled with trivial thoughts and emotions. We may feel embarrassed to realize what kind of thoughts and feelings were filling up our mind. When you think about where they all came from, you will find that most of them arose out of our own doubts and distress.

83

Without exception, we all have our own issues and problems that we have to deal with. If you can't think of any problems that you're facing, then that's probably the problem: you probably have no clue about what's going on in your life. In principle, we all face issues that trouble our mind.

There is absolutely no point in competing over the number or the level of the problems we face in life. If you feel that you have an exceptionally difficult problem that no one else has, you're actually buying into a very egotistical way of thinking. There are plenty of people out there who are agonizing over the same problems as yours. Believing that you are suffering from a problem more than anyone else is simply a sign of arrogance and ignorance. The problems we face are never unique to us. Many people are going through the same distress as we are. They face the same situation or circumstances as we do. Once we realize this, we need to thoroughly examine our current state of mind in a new light. This is one approach to shifting our perspective.

Our anguish is actually caused by our habit of holding onto and constantly mulling over our problems out of the belief that doing so will help us solve them. Being human, we all face problems in life, but the level of our emotional distress is largely due to how we react to and handle them.

When you feel distressed, try dividing your problems into two groups—the ones that you can solve by thinking them over, and those that you can't solve, no matter how much you rack your brain. Or instead, you could sort them into three categories: problems that you can solve right away, those that require a certain length of time to solve, and those that you'll never be able to solve on your own.

You don't have to anguish over the ones that you cannot solve right away, and it's probably easier to give up on the ones that you know that no amount of thinking will ever solve. But most problems fall into the grey area of the ones you can solve with the passing of time. The problems in this group often become the root of anguish. And in most cases, if you ponder deeply, you will find that it is your anxiety about the uncertainty of what will happen that is tormenting you. Most of our distresses come from not knowing how the current situation will unfold: whether the current problem will be solved in three months, six months, or one year down the line, and whether the outcome will be favorable. So the key here is to resolve our anxiety about not knowing how

85

things will develop over time.

So how can we resolve this anxiety? Let's consider how we can deal with the problems in each of the three categories I mentioned. There are problems we cannot solve, no matter how much we think about them. For example, there's no way that I could become the president of the United States at this moment. So if this were something that I wanted, I would simply have to accept that it is not going to happen.

Then there are problems that can be solved quickly. For example, suppose I am giving a lecture and want to end it right away, but I still have forty-five minutes left. This is a problem I can solve in forty-five minutes, so there is no point in worrying about it. These are the first two types of problem.

The third type of problem is the one that is probably the most difficult to handle. For example, at my organization, Happy Science, I have certain measures and plans that I would like to implement for our activities over the next two years. And I also have personal goals related to writing books and teaching and spreading the Truths that I would like to achieve in the next few years. Although I know that I will find a way within the next few years, I cannot take care of all of these things right away. For me, these are the kinds of issues that belong in the grey area.

Once we identify the challenges we are facing, we can assess them and find ways to deal with them. There are several ways to do this, but the most important point is not to be seized by anxiety.

3

How to Find
the Source of Confidence

Accumulating Small Successes

How can we avoid feeling completely dominated by
our fears? By trusting ourselves. We can overcome
anxiety when we cultivate the confidence to know
that we will make it through the challenges we face.

There are two sources of self-confidence. We discover the first source of confidence when we realize
that we will be able to solve any problems that may
come up in the future because we have overcome the
many different problems that came up against us
in the past. If we look back on our past, we should
be able to see that we've made it through every difficulty we've faced so far. Since we have managed to
get through these difficulties, we should be able to

find a way out of whatever circumstances the future presents to us.

The basis of this self-confidence is the accumulation of small victories and successes. This is the key to overcoming the insecurities and uncertainties that we will face in the future. Our past successes help us resolve our current anxiety over the issues that we feel uncertain about. In the same way, we can prepare ourselves for our future insecurities by building up small successes now. And with each step we take, we need to recognize the progress we have made.

As we accumulate small successes, we can build up resistance against anxiety about the unknown future. So the first source of confidence is knowing that we made it through yesterday and the day before; that we have overcome all kinds of problems over the past year, five years, or ten years; and that we were able to overcome each crisis by drawing on our own abilities, believing in our state of mind, and trusting in our friends and the people around us.

Experiencing Our Divine Nature

The second source of self-confidence is an awareness of our divine nature—a firm conviction that we are children of God. We become more confident when we grasp the truth of our existence as children of God.

Looking back at my life, I see how this realization became the basis of my confidence. In 1981, I discovered the existence of the spirit world and experienced it firsthand. This experience was the origin of my firm conviction that I am a child of God, and this conviction gave me confidence. Because of this conviction, I was able to develop an unshakable mind that remained undisturbed even while I was going through a lot of difficult experiences as a member of society.

Many of you who picked up this book probably believe that you are a child of God, but still, a thin layer of doubt will remain until you experience it yourself. And meditation is a way to remove this doubt. Through meditation practice, we concentrate the mind in a way that enables us to directly experience the truth of our existence as children of God.

The meditation practice that I would like to recommend is not something that requires you to retreat to a cave; rather, it is a practical method that you can apply in your day-to-day life. This practice will help you develop an unshakable mind and overcome any anxieties you may have about the future.

So there are basically two ways we can build self-confidence and overcome anxiety about the unknown future: accumulating small victories and gaining awareness as a child of God. An accumulation of small successes requires us to acquire skills, knowledge, and know-how appropriate to this world. While this is one way of building confidence, what I would like to emphasize from my standpoint as a spiritual teacher is the importance of gaining awareness as a child of God. This awareness or conviction is the key to a successful meditation, which is about gradually strengthening your mind's ability to remain unshakable and undisturbed in your everyday life in this hectic society.

4

The Purpose of Meditation

Yoga and Zen have become quite popular these days, and this trend may have led you to pick up this book. Many people who practice meditation believe that it will bring spiritual values into their lives. Some may have decided to start meditating simply because they intuitively knew that it would be a worthwhile practice. And others may have begun meditating thinking that it would help them solve their problems somehow.

So what is the essence of meditation, and what exactly happens when we practice meditation? For what purpose should we practice meditation? I would like to take this opportunity to answer these questions.

As I mentioned in chapter 1, the Japanese word for meditation, *meiso*, literally means "to shut the eyes and think." The first part, *mei*, means "to shut the eyes." The second part, *so*, means "to think." This word precisely describes how we should practice meditation.

Why should we shut our eyes? The purpose of shutting the eyes is to block out the outside world or the third-dimensional material world in which we live. Shutting our eyes cuts us off from the worldly vibrations of this physical world and, at the same time, stops us from influencing the material world's vibrations. The first thing we have to do when we meditate is block out all outside influences. This is the purpose of closing the eyes.

What about the second part of the word for meditation—"to think"? Thinking, in this sense, does not simply refer to the thoughts that pass through our mind throughout the day. Those thoughts come in and out of our minds like waves lapping onto the shore. The type of thinking we want to do in meditation is something deeper. It involves penetrating the depths of the mind, even to the level of the subconscious.

Thinking is also a creative act. When we further deepen the level of our thinking, our *thoughts* become our *will*. The will possesses a physical force. Thoughts are not as concentrated as the will is, so they have no material power. A thought is an idea with a particular direction and a specific goal that makes sense within a certain range of possibilities. Although thoughts are more abstract than the will is, they often have a storyline; they are consistent and structured. This is the type of thinking we want to practice in meditation.

Meditation, then, involves blocking out worldly, physical influences and exploring the inner self. When we meditate, we draw the drapes and shutter the window to the outside world so that we can contemplate the diverse possibilities of our minds.

In that sense, it doesn't matter where we meditate. Whether we have withdrawn to the mountains, retreated to a cave, or stayed in the city, we can meditate the moment we block out worldly vibrations and come face to face with our inner self. Exploring the self in this manner is the way of meditation.

We also use the Sanskrit word *dhyana* (*zenjo* in Japanese) to refer to meditation. *Dhyana* has a Buddhist ring to it, and it refers to a more specific type of meditation. *Dhyana* places more emphasis on concentrating one's mind. And in that sense, we can understand *dhyana* as a practice of removing the peripheral part of our life—all the nonessential elements that are attached to our essential self—and building a pillar at the center of our mind that connects us straight to God. Meditation in general is about exploring the diverse possibilities and creativity of the mind, and *dhyana* is one way of doing that—one type of meditation.

Meditation lets us explore the workings of the mind to pursue a particular goal. One active aspect of meditation is unleashing the mind's creative abilities. We can use meditation to actively pursue our vision and to improve ourselves as we seek to make our dreams come true. In this sense, meditation is a method we can use to explore the diverse possibilities of the mind. In the next few sections, I would like to discuss the essence of some of the basic meditation practices that expand the possibilities of our mind.

95

5

Spontaneity Meditation:
Finding Our True Self
in the Freedom of Nature

⤛✦⤜

The first meditation I would like to discuss is spontaneity meditation—meditation to abandon artifice
and accept things as they are. This meditation practice helps us attain an unfettered mind in which the
mind flows freely, like clouds or a river.

The mind often gets bound by various thoughts
and feelings that make everything more complicated
than it needs to be. Many of us spend all our time
thinking about how to undo the tangled thoughts
and feelings that we have created on our own.

Imagine a flowing stream. In the middle of the
stream is a stake that is snagging pieces of wood,
withered leaves, and debris and gradually stemming
the flow of the stream. We can probably think of

many different ways to make it flow again. The most straightforward solution would be to remove the stake so that it no longer catches debris. But some people try to approach it in a roundabout way and come up with other more complicated methods. For example, they might try to increase the volume of water to flush out the debris. Or they might suggest changing the course of the stream or even dredging it to get rid of the debris. But in the end, the easiest way is to remove the stake so that debris will no longer get caught and block the flow of the stream. Instead of thinking about how to deal with the debris, we should think about how to avoid accumulating and retaining debris in the first place.

Likewise, it is important to maintain a state of mind that flows freely every day. How can we attain a free state like an unobstructed, flowing stream? We do so by figuring out what has brought the obstacles and impatience into our mind in the first place. If we ponder deeply, we find that the roots of these obstacles are our feelings of frustration. It is our dissatisfaction with our current self—perhaps our job performance or achievement, others' evaluation or recognition of our work, or our income or position in our organization. When we cannot attain what we believe we are entitled to, we create obstacles that limit the freedom of the mind.

Spontaneity meditation lets us become who we are, naturally and freely, with no pretense. It reminds us that we human beings are beautiful and precious just as we are. It reminds us of the essential worth of our existence. We don't have to do something extraordinary to prove that we are great. We are shining brightly and wonderfully just as we are, as human beings, as children of God. Suffering arises when we forgot this.

The cause of our suffering is a discord between our desired goal and our current reality. We become impatient and irritated when we feel that we deserve more than we have, and we feel distressed when we try but fail to get what we want. We may be creating our own problems. So we need to ask whether our sufferings are rooted in a misconception of our true self. This is the Taoist teaching of unconditioned spontaneity, of finding our original self.

When we discover the true worth of our mind, we will see that we are not trapped in a place we feel we need to escape from. We will find our shining self, as brilliant as a diamond, right where we find ourselves now. But often we lose sight of our diamond-like nature and instead focus on the dirt and dust attached to the surface. We must know what's most important. When we know that our essential self is shining like a diamond, dirt or dust on the surface is such a trifle that it can be blown away by a puff of air; it will come off sooner or later. So, contemplate why you feel rushed and impatient. Focus on expanding the breadth of your mind, and build confidence in who you are, just as you are.

When we create our own image of what we want to be, we often pursue what people around us think is ideal, not what will illuminate and maximize our true potential. We pursue other people's ideals and often feel frustrated and grumble when we don't live up to them.

We can in fact find our ideal self, or how we should be, in Mother Nature. Taoism asks us to look at Mother Nature when we lose sight of our true nature. Nature does not try to embellish itself. Rivers keep flowing. A meadow spreads before our eyes. Trees keep growing. Birds fly free in the sky. Fish frolic in the water. They engage with life as it is, with nothing to hold them back.

In Mother Nature, we find that all plants live in the circumstances they were given. A violet does not demand any explanation for its color or shape. A violet does not say that it wants to be a dahlia or a tulip; it simply blooms with a radiant and dauntless beauty. Do we humans not feel embarrassed when we compare how they live with how we live?

This philosophy of Taoism is certainly one way of finding our true self. We can find our ideal self as children of God, as creations of God, in nature. All the things in nature embody God's ideals just as they are, so why do we humans create our own suffering by thinking that we need to embellish ourselves to match false ideals? Perhaps this comes from our inflated sense of superiority as human beings. Taoism teaches that we need to free ourselves from this illusion.

This broad perspective definitely helps us examine the essential nature of human beings, but it does not cover every aspect of human life. If the way of nature were all there is to life, we would be left with no human activities. The Taoist perspective does not explain why particular past civilizations flourished or why the human race has been striving to make progress throughout history.

Human suffering may be small in the eyes of nature, but the act of freeing the mind from the fetters and shackles that bind it is invaluable. Meditation is a great tool for doing this. Through the practice of spontaneity meditation, we can think about what it is that's holding us back.

Meditation to
Become One with Nature

When is the last time you looked up at the sky and gazed at floating clouds? When is the last time you enjoyed the murmuring of a brook?

If you live in a big city, it may be years since you took the time to look at the sky or sit near a brook. We often lose sight of this inner contentment, not even realizing what we've lost.

Serenity of mind can be achieved by living freely and artlessly, like clouds floating in the sky or water flowing through a stream.

TRY THIS OUT

102

Becoming the Floating Clouds

♦ Cultivate a rich heart like the clouds floating in the sky. Visualize yourself as an abundant, natural self without any problems or schemes that trouble your mind.

♦ In your meditation, picture yourself among floating clouds. Clouds in the sky don't have any destination. They move wherever the breeze takes them under the sunlight.

♦ Become the clouds in the autumn sky. You are the abundant and encompassing clouds floating slowly and gently as you embrace everything around you. You feel no grudges, no hatred, no anger, and no attachment.

*   *   *   *   *

This is the pure state of mind that humans originally had. Regaining this state of mind is all we need to do to return to heaven.

103

Becoming a Flowing Stream

♦ Now visualize flowing water. Imagine becoming the water of a brook melting into its murmurs and floating downstream. Flow freely, naturally, purely, and artlessly.

♦ A brook does not try to control the speed of the water. It speeds up when the water goes through narrow points, rapids, or the shallows, and it slows down when it enters a wide river.

♦ As a brook, you shelter a variety of underwater plants and animals, and you feel the rhythm of their life inside you.

♦ You are simply flowing with a pure, immaculate, free, and detached mind. Never losing steam, you keep on flowing abundantly, with no plans or strategies.

♦ Imagine yourself without any shackles or fetters that bind you. All you have to do is to imagine yourself flowing continually.

Becoming a Refreshing Breeze

♦ Now you are a refreshing breeze in May, blowing throughout the world.

♦ When you pass by, azalea flowers smile at you, expressing their joy at feeling the breeze. You are the May breeze that carries the sweet scent of azalea.

♦ When you blow, the scent reaches people, bringing smiles to their faces. You are the breeze that carries the fragrance of richness and the scent of nobility throughout the world.

*   *   *   *   *

Even if we can't live in nature, we can still train our mind to experience nature's greatness. Become clouds in the meditation on floating clouds, water in the meditation on a flowing stream, and wind in the meditation on a May breeze.

You'll discover a wonderful world that you've never realized exists and experience the freedom of your soul. You will regain your original, true self, not bound by anything, and experience happiness that lasts forever.

6

Contentment Meditation:
Discovering Our Blessings

Another way to remove mental obstacles is by practicing the meditation of knowing contentment. This meditation helps us examine our current circumstances to see whether we're taking anything for granted. We humans are blessed with many things. If you look back at your own life, you will find many blessings.

But since there is no definite way of comparing our own blessings and happiness with those of others, it is left up to each of us to assess and determine the value of our blessings. For example, do you feel blessed that you're reading this book at this moment? If you think little of the opportunity that you have been given in coming across this book, then that opportunity is indeed insignificant. But you might instead think that reading a book like this and learning the Truths is an absolutely irreplaceable opportunity that is worth more than the status of royalty or nobility, as the Chinese Buddhist monk Huiguo said.

When we consider our current situation from the perspective of knowing contentment, we may feel that discovering and living in the world of Truths is all we ever need to find happiness. Ask yourself, "Why do I want to have a good reputation? Why do I want status or prestige? Why do I want to be respected? Why do I want to look successful? Why do I want compliments from my friends, boss, and coworkers?"

Some people will never be satisfied until they have everything they want. These people want to acquire every single thing that is considered valuable in this world. But we must be aware of an opposite way of living; that is, to discover everything in one thing. While some may say that we can never know the world God created unless we travel to every corner of the globe, there are others, such as the poet William Blake, who could see God's world in a single flower. This is not a privilege reserved for the select few like him; each of us is blessed with the eyes to discover such values. By knowing contentment, we can discover things of absolute value.

107

We often underestimate things of true value because we become so preoccupied with what we want to achieve or gain in this world. When you encounter the Truths and start learning them, trivial things like whether you will get promoted a year ahead of or a year behind your peers should no longer matter at all. If you fear that learning the Truths will stand in your way of promotion, then it may simply mean that your understanding of the Truths is not deep enough.

My understanding of contentment is discovering everything in one thing. Contentment is about finding one value in this world through which you can discover the entire world God created and weaving that absolute value into every aspect of your life.

Being content does not mean compromising with less than we need or being moderate in what we do. It means finding the path to God in everything that exists in this world. Thus, it is important that we discover and embrace the glory of God in what we are already given.

Instead of looking for something you can gain from outside you, look within. There, you will find the part of you that is dearly loved by God. Develop a complete love and faith in that beloved part of you. This will lead you to contentment.

Contemplation on
Finding Contentment

1. Straighten your back and harmonize your breathing.

2. Place your hands together In prayer.

3. Focus your mind so that it will stay right in the middle of your body, where your hands are clasped in prayer.

4. Take several deep breaths.

5. Contemplate the questions on the following pages.

109

♦ *Do you feel any dissatisfaction arising from desires*
that you cannot appease? What are the things
that you want and are frustrated that you cannot
have?

....
....
....
....
....
....
....
....
....
....
....
....
....

♦ *Find the cause of your frustration or dissatisfaction by asking yourself why you feel the way you do.*

....

....

....

....

....

....

....

111

....

....

....

....

....

....

....

♦ *Think about what made you happy or thrilled when you were little. Try to remember things that touched your heart.*

....
....
....
....
....
....
....
....
....
....
....
....
....

♦ *Try to find happiness in the smallest things—for example, the fact that you are alive today, that you are healthy, or that you have a family.*

....

....

....

....

....

....

....

....

....

....

....

....

....

113

Tips for finding contentment:

► Try not to seek recognition for more than what you have worked for. When you begin to receive more recognition than your effort has merited, a heart of conceit grows within you and leads you to the wrong path.

► When you work very hard to achieve your goal, the way to be happy is to be content with a 10 percent return for the 100 percent of the effort you've made. You will feel grateful and happy because you will be offering the remaining 90 percent of your work to God. You are not giving back to God if you received 100 percent returns on your effort.

114

7

Relationship Harmony Meditation:

Cultivating Understanding

There are things we don't have complete control over, and among them are the feelings and thoughts of others. When I talk in front of an audience, I can influence them to a certain extent, but I cannot force them to change what they think or how they feel. I cannot take control of what others think throughout the day. I may be able to make an impact on their life, but that's about all I can do.

Each and every one of us has a kingdom within the mind. We are the sole master of this kingdom, and no one else can control it. Our ability to take control of the kingdom within is truly invaluable, but at the same time, we sometimes suffer when we find ourselves unable to control the kingdom within other people's minds.

Often, the root of our suffering lies in the existence of other people, as the Japanese Buddhist monk Nichiren said. If we lived completely alone, we would not have many of the distresses that we experience in life. Reading this, you may say to yourself, "Then we should just stay away from other people." But then there would be no spiritual growth for our souls. The existence of others is a crucial element in the development of our souls. But with it comes distress and suffering. So human relationships have both positive and negative aspects.

What we can do on our end to improve our relationships is shift our perspective and look at the positive side of other people's existence. For example, it may come as a shock if someone criticizes you, but you can still benefit from the experience. At the very least, it puts you on your mettle. It also shows that you are not perfect, so it may help you develop humility.

We also need to perceive others in the right way, and at the same time, we have to have an accurate perception of how others see us. So what is the right way to see others? It is to observe others in a calm, objective way. And think about these questions: Why is the other person bringing this discord into our relationship? Why does he or she keep doing or saying everything I hate?

When you ponder these questions, you will find that you don't have a complete understanding of the other person. You may not feel fully understood yourself, but you can recognize that you don't fully understand the other person either.

We often don't think about the fact that we misunderstand others and instead focus on how much other people misunderstand us. You may feel that others understand only 10 percent of who you are. Or you may feel their understanding of you is 50 percent. But can you answer the question of how much you understand others? Do you have a 100 percent understanding of others? Could it be 50 percent? You may find it difficult to answer these questions with any certainty.

Consider a relationship you have that has become difficult. If you think about it deeply, you will find that you and the other person actually don't understand each other that well. And this misunderstanding between you is not entirely the other person's fault; you are partly responsible for it, too.

At the very least, if you feel that you don't completely understand the other person, you cannot expect that person to completely understand you. This should be the basis of how you see a relationship. Just as there are certain aspects of you that others cannot see, there are things about that person that you are not aware of.

We can't always evaluate others by the same standard we use to judge ourselves. Other people may appear imperfect to our eyes, but we appear imperfect to their eyes, too. There may be someone that you think is the worst person alive, but not everyone feels the same way about him or her. Some people may get along well with that person. This means that they see goodness in the person you resent so much.

If you are reading this book, you probably have an interest in spiritual Truths. In that sense, you are a seeker of Truths and may well have a spiritually advanced soul. And when you see gangsters or beggars, you may pity them for having taken the wrong path in life. And indeed they may have taken the wrong path in life, but it is also true that you are not really seeing goodness in them.

It may be difficult for you to see positive qualities in a beggar or gangster, but other beggars and gangsters can see this goodness in one another. Some beggars are held in higher regard than others. There are beggars whose magnetic personalities win the respect of others. Others are well thought of because they pay close attention to the opinions of others. And some beggars probably have good reasons to beg.

Similarly, some gangsters take good care of their peers. Some are respected for their big-brotherly affection for their younger fellows—they may give advice and even risk their lives to save others. They see the goodness in one another, in their own world. And in fact, there may actually be good people among them. But often, we assume that they are all wrong, that they are completely mistaken, and that their minds are distorted.

I am now in a position to teach spiritual Truths, but let's suppose that I cannot see the goodness in Beggars A and B, but Beggar C can see their goodness. In that case, I am inferior to Beggar C in that respect, and I need to reflect on myself and think about why I can't see their goodness.

As this example implies, there are many different ways of seeing other people. It is often the feeling that we know better than others that leads us to develop an unforgiving heart. On the other hand, we develop forgiveness by knowing everything about others and tolerance by recognizing that we don't always have a complete understanding of others. When we adopt this perspective, we can start to harmonize our relationships with others.

Other people are unique masterpieces created by

God. Consider a famous painting. People have all kinds of opinions about it. Some love it, while others hate it. You might prefer some paintings to others, even if they are all works of the same artist. Yet each work shines with its own unique value and beauty. If you don't like a particular painting, it is not necessarily the artist's fault; it may just be that you don't have an eye to appreciate its beauty. With this perspective in mind, you can no longer claim that a painting has no value just because you don't like it.

Understanding diverse values is the basis of tolerance and forgiveness. Some people overlook others' mistakes simply out of indecisiveness or weakheartedness. Although they may appear forgiving, their attitude is different in nature from the forgiveness that we can cultivate by recognizing that we do not know everything about others and trying to understand them more completely.

Visualizing
Relationship Harmony

Having a talk with someone you are having a problem with can be quite difficult. So start the dialogue in your mind first, while wishing to make it a reality. This is a very effective practice that anyone can use to improve interpersonal relationships. Try practicing this visualization for ten to fifteen minutes every day. Then, one day, quite unexpectedly, you will be able to restore and harmonize your relationship with that person.

TRY THIS OUT

121

♦ Visualize someone with whom you are having difficulty, and try to harmonize the relationship in your mind. Think of positive words you can say to that person; you can even say them out loud.

....
....
....
....
....
....
....
....
....
....
....
....
....
....

♦ Relax your mind, and visualize their lives getting better and better. Imagine your relationship with them improving. This is a spiritual practice you can carry out on your own.

....
....
....
....
....
....
....
....
....
....
....
....
....
....

Meditating on a harmonized relationship is actually about having a dialogue with the guardian spirit of the person with whom you are having the problem. Your thoughts will actually reach the person through his or her guardian spirit. Guardian spirits receive the thoughts we send to the people they are protecting, and they try to give proper guidance accordingly.

We can also harmonize relationships with others by vividly visualizing, every day, how they can improve their lives and become happier and happier.

*   *   *   *   *

124

8

Self-Realization Meditation:
Fulfilling God's Ideals

Self-realization meditation helps us improve ourselves and make progress in life. This kind of meditation can also be the basis for a life filled with happiness. But when we practice meditation for self-improvement and success, we must make sure that we have the right motivation and goal and that we are not starting off from the wrong place or taking the wrong path.

I once said that self-realization should not be about fulfilling your personal desires or achieving worldly success.* It should not only be about making the most out of your talent or abilities either. Our self-realization should bring us closer to God's ideal.

---

* See chapter 5, "The Principle of Progress," in Ryuho Okawa, *The Science of Happiness* (Vermont: Destiny Books, 2009).

Let's look at a simple example. Suppose you dream of becoming a spiritual teacher who speaks in front of a large audience. You are a good speaker and have a lot of life experiences to share, and you are confident that you can give a good talk on spiritual Truths for an hour or two. This may be how you want to achieve your self-realization, but you have to ask if this will contribute to the self-realization of the people listening to your talk. Although your speech may seem impressive to those who are encountering the Truths for the first time, if your aim is to give the talk to a group of people devoted to studying the Truths, you may not yet be qualified to teach. We need to be able to make this kind of assessment to avoid choosing a wrong path in life.

We face similar situations in different contexts. Let's say you volunteer at a seminar event. There are many types of work for volunteers at this event, including book selling, reception, and security. You want to volunteer at the reception desk where others can see you easily, but to your disappointment you are assigned to work security at the back of the stage. You may feel that you are suited for a receptionist because you are really good with people, but that's not where you are assigned.

This may sound like a trifling matter, but this kind of thing might frustrate you. At times like this, we need to remind ourselves not to let our small personal goals limit our perspective. Remember, we are aiming for a much bigger ideal—God's ideal—and we are volunteers in the service of God. Our ultimate goal should be to realize God's ideals, not to fulfill our personal desires.

When you take part in a spiritual or religious movement with a mistaken perspective, you might find yourself wanting to take advantage of the movement for your own self-realization or to make a name for yourself in this world. For example, seekers of Truths often have a strong desire to become an angel of light. They often join religious or spiritual organizations hoping that someone will see God's light emanating from them and recognize that they are actually angels on earth. But it's small-minded to think that that's all you need to live a life of happiness.

The basis of your self-realization should be a good understanding of what you can do, as a volunteer for God, to help realize God's high ideals. Of course, I, too, have personal goals I would like to achieve, but I always ask myself whether my decisions and actions

127

are in service to God. It is when we lose this perspective that we take the wrong path. Although this may sound harsh, the moment you seek self-realization only to take advantage of or show off your authority, your spiritual growth comes to a halt; you are only a step away from falling off a cliff.

I cannot emphasize enough the importance of understanding the true purpose of self-realization. In fact, self-realization in the truest sense is not possible unless it accords with God's will. God created everything in this world. He created the grand universe in which our planet Earth exists. You were born into one of the countries on this comparatively small planet. And you now live in one of the towns in that country and are reading this book in a small corner of that town. Always remember where you stand in relation to the grand scheme of existence. Don't forget that you are now walking in the hand of the Almighty God. Don't wander around aimlessly; instead, strive to do God's work.

Three Keys to Successful
Self-Realization Meditation

1. Bringing Happiness to People Around You

We experience true joy when other people rejoice in our success. When you visualize your wishes coming true, first imagine how your success will bring happiness to those who helped you achieve your dream.

2. Improving Your Character

Think about whether your self-realization will contribute to your inner growth. Our self-realization should not be merely about satisfying our own personal desires. True self-realization should improve our character so that we can help, guide, and encourage many people to walk a path to happiness.

3. Being in Service to God

Realizing that, ultimately, we are here to serve and fulfill the will of God will lead us to accomplish great things. Devoting our whole life to God is the highest form of self-realization. In your meditation, visualize yourself achieving your highest form of self-actualization as a servant of God.

129

9

Seeing Ourselves
from the Minuscule Perspective
and the Cosmic Perspective

130

While meditating, we may sometimes experience our consciousness expanding to the scale of the grand universe. But this does not necessarily prove the greatness of our souls. Regardless of whether we have this kind of experience, we have a mission to fulfill as human beings living in this world. Each of us has a unique mission, and our destination in the after-world will be determined by how much of our role we were able to fulfill in service to God's will.

Unfortunately, many spirits have taken the wrong path and have ended up in the world of hell because they misunderstood their role in this world. They made the grave mistake of neglecting their role in this miniature garden that God has created and letting their egos take control, as if they ruled the universe. Our self-centered desire to have everyone else do as we wish breeds arrogance and gives rise to this error of the mind. So we have to know our place as part of the whole, as one member of the flock. But at the same time, we have to remember that as children of God, we are sacred beings, and that infinite light exists within each of us.

We need to see ourselves from both the grand, cosmic perspective and the small, individual perspective. When we feel insignificant, petty, or worthless, we have to remind ourselves of our magnificence as children of God. But when we feel proud of our worldly success and feel as if we can control others as we please, we have to realize how small our existence is in the context of the grand universe.

Seeing ourselves from these two opposite perspectives is essential to seeing ourselves rightly in our practices of introspection and meditation. The minuscule perspective helps us discover God's light shining within us, while the cosmic perspective helps us realize the smallness of our existence in the vast panorama of the grand universe. When we examine ourselves and our way of life from these two perspectives, we will discover the true essence of meditation.

Chapter 3

Q & A
on
Meditation

1

How to Meditate
When We Are Fatigued

134

Question:

When we are not feeling well, is it better to meditate or to refrain from meditating? What kind of meditation should we do when we are not in good physical condition?

Answer:

When you are physically exhausted, I recommend that you regain your strength before meditating. If you feel completely drained after work, get some rest, relax your body, and try to recharge your spiritual energy. Often, when we're feeling extremely tired, we've been affected by the rough vibrations of the different kinds of people we've met during the day. Our physical condition has a lot to do with our mental exhaustion. So try relieving your fatigue before meditating.

If the cause of your fatigue is lack of sleep, get some sleep. If you're not getting enough sleep during the weekdays, use the weekends to catch up on your sleep. Planning your sleep schedule and making it into a habit is also important. Another cause of physical fatigue is lack of exercise. If you haven't been working out, it's a good idea to start training your body.

Our physical condition has a big impact on our meditation practice. If we practice meditation when we are in bad condition, we may end up receiving negative influences from stray spirits. For that reason, I also recommend refraining from meditating when intoxicated.

Often, when we're feeling extremely tired, we've been affected by the rough vibrations of the different people we've met during the day. I had to deal with this issue back when I was working at a trading company. I was exposed to various negative thought energies coming from people around me. Fortunately, I no longer have this problem, because I now live in very favorable circumstance for meditation, which allows me to keep my mind undisturbed. When our mind is disturbed by outside influences, we can't communicate with the heavenly spirits. With an untuned mind, we are likely to attract negative spirits.

But there may be times when you feel that you need to meditate, no matter what your condition is. You may want to meditate at a particular time even though you are not feeling well, because you have no other time to meditate. For example, if you come home late every day throughout the whole year, it will be difficult to find time to meditate. So what should you do when you can't change your physical condition but want to meditate anyway? I recommend practicing the breathing exercise to quiet your mind. The breathing exercise is the simplest way to regulate the mind's vibrations. Try taking deep breaths in and out, and see if you can concentrate your mind.

There is no specific posture we need to take when meditating. We don't have to sit cross-legged, but we should always sit up straight. Then, take a few deep breaths and see if you feel recharged or feel energy filling you up inside. The breathing practice alone can often get rid of haziness and fatigue. When we breathe in deeply from the mouth, we can absorb the various positive energies that pervade the great universe.

Try breathing using the lower abdominal muscles below the navel. We have many chakras in our body, but the main center of our spiritual energy is located in the lower abdominal area. Deep breathing regulates the energy in this main chakra, allowing us to harmonize our mind's vibrations. So try recharging your energy through deep breathing, and then you'll be able to receive light from heaven. This simple exercise will help you attain peace of mind.

You can do the deep breathing practice anywhere —not only at home, but also at work. When you find yourself getting irritated and your mind is disturbed, you can calm your mind simply by breathing from the lower abdomen. If you feel like lashing out at someone, breathe in deeply while focusing on your lower abdomen. This will help you harmonize your physical energy. As you do this, you will start receiving light from your guardian and guiding spirits in heaven; you will feel the light flowing into you.

The more spiritual you become, the more receptive you will be to this light. You will be able to receive light flowing from above just by practicing deep breathing. When you receive divine light, you will feel a sense of warmth filling your chest area down to your belly. This is something you can experience simply by breathing deeply.

So when you are not in good physical condition, it's probably safe to practice the deep-breathing exercise. Try this first, and if you'd like to do more meditation, you can try the practice of visualizing the full moon. If you are extremely exhausted, I recommend limiting yourself to deep breathing and visualizing the full moon. That way, you will probably not be influenced by negative spirits.

If your body starts shaking a lot during meditation, it often means that you are under the influence of a negative spirit. This phenomenon also occurs when you are about to open a channel to the spirit world, but that rarely happens. If your body starts shaking too much—back and forth or side to side — stop meditating. Turn on the light or go to a well-lit place and practice meditation with your eyes open. Meditating in a well-lit place can help you avoid receiving negative spiritual influences.

You can also take a pencil and paper and write down your thoughts. Try different types of meditation—such as the contemplation on finding contentment and visualizing relationship harmony (see chapter 2)—with your eyes open and while writing down your thoughts.

When you are not feeling well, especially when you are mentally unstable, I recommend limiting yourself to practicing introspective meditation. I suggest avoiding self realization meditation, in which you visualize the goals and dreams you would like to achieve. If you find it difficult to meditate on self-reflection, it usually means you are physically exhausted, so you probably want to rest first.

Our body and mind are one, so it is important to harmonize both. We cannot solve every problem simply by controlling our state of mind. We have to improve both our physical condition and our mental state. Sometimes, lack of nutrition is the cause of our fatigue. To improve our physical condition, we need to eat plenty of nutritious food, exercise, and get ample sleep. We should only enter a deep state of meditation after we have improved our physical condition. This is my prescription for those who want to practice meditation in the midst of a busy, modern lifestyle.

2

How Visualization Works

Question:

I have a difficult time visualizing my wish. Does this mean my mind is clouded? What can I do to see a clear vision during meditation?

141

It doesn't necessarily mean that your mind is clouded. It could be that your wish isn't strong enough. You may feel that you need to see a clear image of what you wish to realize, but it could be that your impetus is simply not that strong. If it's something you absolutely want, you should be able to vividly see the image in your mind.

Suppose you are an outside sales representative. Your job requires you to drive to visit your customers, but you don't own a car. In this situation, you should be able to vividly visualize having a car. However, if you live in a city with a good public transportation system, you may not need a car for your job. You may still wish to own a car, but if you don't feel a strong need for one, you may only have a vague image of owning a car, and thus may not be able to visualize it clearly.

In the same way, if your situation requires you to own a house in the suburbs, you should be able to visualize such a house clearly. But if you are basically happy with where you live and only vaguely wish to move someday, you probably won't be able to see a clear vision of the house you want. So, whether or not you can see a vivid image often depends on how strong your need is. A strong desire is one of the keys to successful visualization.

Another point I would like to make is that, while visualization is quite popular, it is not the only way to make your wishes come true. For example, many of my wishes have come true without my ever having to visualize them vividly. I usually have brief thoughts about the things I wish to happen and then set these ideas aside. The images that have flashed through my mind have almost always come true after a while, usually within a few years.

The secret to this is that I can freely communicate with my guardian and guiding spirits, and they know all my thoughts. Whenever I have a vision, I ask them to make it come true when the time is right, and then I set the idea aside until it comes true. If you establish this connection with your guardian and guiding spirits, you no longer have to vividly visualize your desires. But since not many people have the spiritual ability to directly communicate with their guardian and guiding spirits, they use visualization to strengthen their mental power.

By holding a strong and clear vision, you can imprint your wishes deeply in your mind. This is

143

how you can reach your guardian and guiding spirits and motivate them to help you fulfill your wish. A strong and vivid vision is a tool you can use to realize your wish, because your earnest wish wins over your guardian and guiding spirits.

To illustrate, let's say there is a project that you really want to be part of. If you keep begging your boss to assign you to that project, your boss will probably let you do it. I'm sure you've experienced something like this, but metaphorically speaking, this is how self-visualization works.

In most cases, we achieve self-realization when we receive spiritual guidance. So as long as you are in a state in which you can constantly receive spiritual guidance from heaven, you don't need a clear vision to attain your heart's desire.

When you are in tune with your guardian and guiding spirits, all you have to do is hold thoughts like, "I wish to speak in public someday. I would like to give lectures," and they will come true in a few years. Several years ago, I thought to myself, "I would like to publish books based on my lectures some day." Now my lectures are getting published one after another. The lectures I'm giving this year will be compiled and published as books next year.

This idea that flashed in my mind some years ago is now becoming reality, even though I didn't have any specific plans to achieve it.

Similarly, back in 1985 when I was working on my first book, *The Spiritual Messages of Nichiren*, I thought it would be nice to meet my readers one day. I never had a clear vision of so many people attending my lectures as do now. I just thought that it would happen when the time came. As you can see, visualization is not the only way to achieve self-realization. I hope that this will help you better understand how self realization works.

3

Dealing with Interruptions during Meditation

Question:

When I meditate, I get easily disturbed by the sound of a phone ringing, a knock on the door, or someone entering the room. Does ending meditation in the middle like this have negative impact on my soul? Is there any proper method or procedure for ending meditation? How should I restart meditation when I am forced to end it abruptly?

Answer:

We certainly do not want to be disturbed during meditation, so we want to avoid things that can interrupt us, especially phones. The phone is the enemy of meditation. And it certainly makes it difficult to meditate when you are surrounded by lots of people, too.

I would like to share a story about a time when I was interrupted while I was in a meditative state. One day, I was having a spiritual interview session with William Shakespeare—I was conveying his messages and recording them for publication as a book.* But I had to interrupt the session right in the middle because a delivery arrived. I heard the doorbell ring, so I stopped the session midway through and went to answer the door. After I received the package, I restarted the session, but Shakespeare was pretty annoyed, because he'd just been getting into the best part of his talk, which was his theory of tragedy in literature. He wasn't angry, but he was no longer in the mood for talking. It took me a while to get him motivated to begin again, and we ended up having to

147

---

* The spiritual interview with William Shakespeare was compiled and published in 1988 in the book *Picasso Reijishu* ("A Collection of Spiritual Messages from Picasso"), by Tsuchiya Shoten. Happy Science republished it in 2006 in volume 39 of *Ryuho Okawa Reigen Zenshu* ("Ryuho Okawa's Complete Collection of Spiritual Messages").

start the session all over again.

I told him that, as a divine spirit, he shouldn't be disturbed by something like this and that he should discipline his mind, but this is an issue that actors and artists like him often have to face. I'm sure they wouldn't like it if the police turned up in the middle of a performance and interrupted the play. So I understand why he wasn't happy to be interrupted in the middle of his talk and lost his motivation.

This is all to say that I understand how difficult it can be to go back to meditation when we are interrupted in the middle. And these interruptions do make it difficult for those of us who live in the material world to communicate with spirits in the other world.

As for your question about whether these interruptions will damage your soul, I think it depends on the individual. But I don't think you should take it too seriously; you can simply let it go and go back to your meditation. If you become too sensitive about it, you'll develop a tendency to avoid people and withdraw from the world. If you feel that you are sensitive, I suggest that you become a little more impervious. I don't think any meditation is so urgent that it needs to be done at that very instant. If you find that you can't harmonize your mind after an interruption, just try again another time.

I know that some people teach that it can be damaging to end meditation abruptly, but I don't think you should be too concerned about that. You can end your meditation session whenever you feel the need to. If you feel you need to do more, you can simply go back to it. In any case, what gets in the way of entering the meditative state is the feeling that you must do it right at this instant. This tension makes it difficult to meditate, so I recommend that you relax and go back to meditation when it feels natural to you.

Shakyamuni Buddha often meditated in the middle of the night to avoid distractions. But if you did this, you would be dozing off at work and wouldn't get any work done. Those of us who have flexible work hours may be able to nap during the day, but most people are not blessed with such a favorable situation for meditating late at night.

If it's difficult for you to meditate at night, you can make use of the morning instead. For instance, you can get up at five or six in the morning and set two hours aside for meditation. It takes a little bit of willpower to get up early, but if you really want to do it, I'm sure you can. You probably won't be inter-

149

rupted in the early morning. So if your challenge is that you get interrupted during the day and at night, I recommend that you meditate in the morning.

You don't have to follow any particular style of meditation. Those who live an inspired life are constantly in a meditative state, and these people often seem absentminded. For example, there's an anecdote about Issac Newton mistaking a pocket watch for an egg, boiling it, and not realizing his mistake until he tried to eat it. Another anecdote about Newton is that when his neighbor's cat had kittens, he made a small passageway for the kittens and a big passageway for the mother. It never occurred to him that the big passageway would serve the kittens just as well. He thought that the kittens could only use a small one, so he made two passageways of different sizes. His ability to deal with reality is questionable, but I think these anecdotes show that he was constantly in a meditative state.

The same was true for Socrates. Socrates apparently stood upright for three or four days right in the middle of a battle. It is incredible how deeply he meditated. He didn't even notice the artillery shells flying around him. I wonder how he managed to avoid getting hit, but it is a famous story that he stood in the middle of a battlefield, unconscious, for whole days and nights.

So another approach to avoiding distraction is to concentrate your mind to the degree that Newton and Socrates did. If you go that far, your environment will no longer interfere with your meditation. But if you do this during work hours, you will probably lose your job, so you should probably only try doing this during your commute and on the weekends.

Most people probably have difficulty setting aside time to meditate every day. If that's the case for you, you can take the time for meditation on the weekends. And keep in mind that you can examine your mind at any time of the day or night. So during the weekdays, you might use the time you spend commuting or the time just before you go to sleep to reflect on your thoughts and actions for the day. You can make a habit of practicing self-reflection during the weekdays and then spending an hour or two each week, on the weekends or holidays, in meditation. For longer meditation sessions, I recommend that you start with self-reflective meditation and then gradually go into a deeper meditative state.

It can be challenging to integrate a meditative practice into an ordinary business life. When I first started my organization, Happy Science, in 1987, I spent most of my time meditating instead of doing office work. But as the organization grew, I could no longer devote all my time to meditation. We began hiring a lot of staff, and it started to feel more like a regular company with more administrative work and paperwork, etc. Once you become involved in tasks that require practical business skills, it becomes very difficult to balance office work with meditation practice.

I shared three keys to meditation in chapter 1 of this book. The first key is to have absolute faith in the existence of God and divine spirits. The second key is to abandon ego and self-interest. The third key is to examine your current self from the perspective of heaven. What do you think would happen if we applied these keys to our everyday business activities?

First, if you started talking about having absolute faith in God and divine spirits at the office, people would start to look at you strangely. People don't usually think about things like this at work. If you tried to practice the second key, abandoning your ego and self-interest, it would probably make it very difficult for you to work in a company that pursues profit. And once you start seeing yourself from the perspective of the other world, it becomes difficult to keep your feet on the ground. This means that businesspeople are basically unable to practice meditation, because all the three keys to meditation end up preventing them from doing their work.

So how should we deal with this issue? I think that we should shift our perspective completely. That is, we need to enhance our work performance to the best of our ability. When we improve our work skills, such as the ability to manage our time, we can create room in our schedule to enter a meditative state.

To live a meditative life, as Newton and Socrates did, while working in a regular business environment, we need to develop the ability to compress the amount of time it takes to do our work. If you can make quick decisions on the issues that you face, even when unexpected work comes up, you can still take care of it in a short period of time. In this way, your mind will always be at ease, even while you are busy at work. This sense of ease, a quiet, passive state within, will create extra room in your mind, which will open you up to receive all kinds of inspiration.

So if we want to be able to go into a meditative state while living a busy life, we need to develop strong practical work skills. We cannot enter a meditative state when we are simultaneously caught up in trying to solve more than two or three problems at a time. That's why it's crucial to develop the ability to solve problems quickly.

No matter what kind of job you have, even if you are an office assistant, if you can improve your work skills to the extent that you can make decisions just as quickly as the president of the company would, you can easily create extra time to relax and go into a meditative state. As a rough guide, you can aim to get an hour's work done in ten minutes, thereby compressing your work so that it takes one-sixth the time.

To start with, try coming up with three solutions to any problem as soon as it arises. Then determine which solution is most viable and put it into practice right away. This is how you can develop the ability to make quick decisions one after another. This ability will help you discern whom to consult on which matter and what you need to do to take care of the issue. You will also be able to decide which matters can wait, so even if you get lots of phone calls in the morning, you can instantaneously decide which ones you can get back to later in the day. In this way, you can switch quickly from one task to another while focusing on what's most important.

It's practically impossible to enter a meditative state if you are so bogged down with work that you are panicking because you don't know how you'll be able to finish it during regular working hours. For example, you may be planning on finishing off work from yesterday, but as soon as you get to the office, you get a phone call about an issue that you need to take care of right away, forcing you to leave yesterday's work undone. This may make you feel lost as to what to do and leave you feeling disorganized.

If you find yourself in this situation, try writing down a list of things that you have to do the first thing in the morning, perhaps with a cup of coffee. If you can come up with ten things that you have to do right away, for example, sort them out in order of priority and then stick that list on your telephone, or wherever you can see it. As you take care of each task, cross it off the list. If you can cross each item off, one after another, and get them all done by the end of the morning, you will be left with no work to do for the rest of the day.

This is how you can reduce the amount of work you have left undone and create extra room in your mind. If you are constantly feeling distressed over unsolved problems, you won't be able to enter a med-

155

itative state. Just like the just-in-time manufacturing method employed by Toyota, in which you produce the product in the most efficient way as soon as you receive an order, you can compress your workload by finishing tasks as soon as they come up.

Your work capability has a lot to do with your meditation practice. If you find yourself constantly distracted by your surroundings, try improving your work skills. If you can get your work done ten times faster, you can have ten times more free time in your day. This will allow you to do a variety of other things besides your job, so please consider how you can apply this technique to your life.

Finally, I would like to note the importance of sending your thoughts in the right direction when you focus your mind. If you use your ability in the wrong way and send your thoughts toward the lower part of the fourth dimension of the spirit world (hell), you will be far from the kind of meditation you want to be practicing. I would like you to be careful about this point when you meditate.

4

To Whom Should We Pray?

Question:

I would like to know to whom we should pray during meditation. Should we pray to a specific spirit, or should we try to visualize the Creator when we pray?

157

Answer:

Essentially, we should be praying to our own guardian spirits. This is because our guardian spirits know us best and know what's best for us. So we should direct our prayer to our guardian spirits.

Our guardian spirits will then assess the content of our prayer. If they feel that the prayer is beyond their capacity to answer, they will seek the assistance of a spirit from a higher dimension. They will bring in an expert who can solve the specific issues that we're praying about. So as a general rule, all prayers should go through our guardian spirits.

In principle, our guardian spirits serve as intermediaries who pass our prayers on to other spirits, but if you have a specific goal in a specialized field, you can pray directly to a divine spirit who has expertise in that area. If you would like to direct your prayer to a particular spirit, angel, god, goddess, or historical figure to achieve a specific purpose, you can do so.

But keep in mind that the power of your prayer correlates with the level of your awareness. So if you pray to the Shinto god Ameno Minakanushino Kami, for example, your prayer will not reach him unless your awareness is on the same level as his. So in this sense, a prayer to the fundamental God of the Universe will most certainly not reach Him. You may direct your prayer to the Creator, but it will take literally forever for it to reach Him.

However, as long as you aim your prayer in the right direction, it will get to someone between you and the spirit you're thinking of. As long as it is a good prayer and you are sending it to the spirit who has the expertise in your area of interest, someone with close ties with that spirit will receive your prayer.

Divine spirits have different areas of expertise. For instance, the Shinto god Okuninushino Kami specializes in granting wishes related to marriage and economic prosperity, so he probably doesn't fulfill wishes to cure illness as much. Florence Nightingale and Edgar Cayce, on the other hand, specialize in healing illnesses. They and other healing spirits become busy when a lot of people in this world direct healing prayers toward them. In any case, which spirit responds to a prayer depends on that prayer—they're delivered case by case—but someone in the same spirit group will receive it.

The spirit who receives your prayer will then examine it carefully, just as a government officer decides whether to approve an application that her office has received. If the spirit approves the prayer, she sends out paperwork, and someone is assigned to answer it. This is when you start receiving a response to your prayer. On the other hand, if the spirit determines that your prayer does not accord with the will of God, she rejects it and sends it back unanswered.

Sending a prayer is like shooting bullets or arrows into the sky. If it doesn't reach its target, it comes falling back to earth and gets lost. There are many unanswered prayers dispersed all over the earth and around the universe. People's unfulfilled wishes are always swirling around us and occasionally affect us in various ways.

In fact, the downside to visiting shrines and temples is that we can easily be influenced by the unfulfilled wishes of people who have prayed there. Unanswered prayers accumulate in these places. For some people, praying is just about trying to make their selfish wishes come true. They send fervent prayers to heaven, but often no one accepts their prayers. These unanswered wishes fall back to earth and sometimes hit the head of the next person to visit the same place.

On the other hand, if a person visiting a temple or shrine is in the right state of mind, or if it is deemed necessary to grant his wish, his prayer will be answered. And when these wishes and prayers accumulate, they start to exert a certain force. As more and more people come together to pray, their wishes—for example, to bring about success and prosperity in business—gradually build up. If their prayers are deemed appropriate, then heavenly spirits from the fourth dimension and above start to respond. Divine spirits that can give guidance to those who are praying will come together and start helping them.

So before you pray, first check your state of mind. Adopt a humble attitude, and carefully examine your wishes. If you find your prayer to be worthy then offer it. In the end, it is up to the spirits in heaven to decide whether to accept your prayer, so I think it is best to leave it up to them. If you keep offering the same prayer over and over, it may mean that it has become an obsession. We need to be careful not to be enthralled by our own desires.

For more information about prayer, please refer to chapter 10, "The Principle of Prayer," in my book *The Science of Happiness* (Vermont: Destiny Books, 2009). I have also discussed the relationship between prayer and the Eightfold Path in chapter 2 of *The Essence of*

Buddha (New York: IRH Press, 2016). As that book explains, Shakyamuni Buddha intended to incorporate prayer into his notions of Right Mindfulness and Right Concentration. I hope that you will find these books helpful in deepening your understanding of prayer.

5

Repelling Negative
Spiritual Influences

Question:

Sometimes, when I put my hands together in prayer at shrines, it feels as though my hands are being pulled up, and when I meditate at night, I often feel an electricity-like shock in my body. One of my friends has told me that he had similar experiences when he was reading one of your books. I can also feel that some people give off bad vibes, which makes me want to avoid them. Can you give me advice as to how I can increase my inner strength so that I can repel these negative influences?

Answer:

Answering these types of questions in public can sometimes be a bit sensitive, because they often involve personal issues. If it were a private consultation, I would be able to give you specific advice, but since this will be published in a book, I can only give you general guidance. I hope you'll understand.

A certain percentage of people experience an electric-shock-like, tingly feeling in their head when they read spiritual books. When you feel this prickling sensation piercing your head, it is usually the spirit of a snake that's causing it. When you feel an electric-shock-like sensation in your shoulders or lower back, it is usually caused by the spirit of a fox. This is what happens when animal spirits have a spiritual influence over you, although the sensation you experience may vary depending on the type of spirit.

Stray animal spirits gather in shrines and temples because they want to be saved. When spiritually sensitive people go to these places and pray, they might feel this electric-shock-like sensation caused by the animal spirits that have gathered there. If they mistake it for a blessing and express gratitude, they can be spiritually bound by these spirits. People who have

164

experienced this kind of sensation are susceptible to these kinds of spiritual influences, so I recommend that they avoid going to places like graveyards, temples, and shrines.

About your friend who experienced a spiritual reaction to my book, please ask him more about the kind of response he had. If he felt warmth around his chest or felt a warm feeling welling up inside that brought tears to his eyes, it was a sign that his guardian spirit was responding. But it wouldn't have been his guardian spirit if his body started moving on its own volition, if he felt a pain in his neck or head, or if he heard ringing in his ears. In extreme cases, some people cannot read the words written in my books. They can flip through a book and see the words on the pages, but they can't comprehend what the words say. Similarly, there are those who attend my lectures but cannot hear anything I say. These people have a lot of things to reflect on.

I would like you to be aware of two different kinds of reactions to spiritual phenomena. If you experience a warm feeling welling up inside, then you are reacting to heavenly spirits. If you experience other types of feelings, such as your feet getting cold or painful, especially at night, that is not a good sign. I suggest that you disregard it and try not to focus your attention on it.

Getting too excited about the various phenomena you experience allows different negative spirits to influence you. So if you experience phenomena that make you think that you are spiritually sensitive or receptive, such as feeling a tingling sensation in your head or a buzzing in the ears, try not to take any more interest in them. Buzzing in the ears is often a sign that various spirits are talking to you. And if you become more spiritually sensitive, you may start hearing their voices, but I strongly advise you not to listen to them.

Those who practice meditation often want to experience spiritual phenomena, so they get excited when they start feeling or hearing things. There should be no problem if these sounds or feelings are coming from a divine spirit, but carefully examine what you are experiencing before you get excited. If you feel no warmth coming from within, you should stop there. Instead of going into a deeper state of meditation, end the meditation session right away.

If you experience negative spiritual phenomena, refrain from entering a meditative state for a while and work on improving your lifestyle. Do your work properly and establish a well-balanced life. Eat a nutritious diet and build up your physical strength. Make sure you get enough sleep, too. Get up early in the morning, and don't stay up late at night. In particular, I would like to advise those who have insomnia and are easily irritated because of lack of sleep to refrain from practicing meditation. It's spiritually dangerous to practice meditation when you are not sleeping well at night. Please know that you cannot receive guidance from divine spirits when you are exhausted from lack of sleep.

It is crucial to establish a healthy lifestyle before practicing meditation. A steady, balanced life is prerequisite to receiving guidance from reliable spirits. If we want to receive guidance from higher spirits, we need to improve our lifestyle even more.

Your body is a barometer of your physical and mental state. If you are always grumbling and dissatisfied, it may be because you are not in good physical condition. If this is the case, make sure you get enough sleep, eat a nutritious diet, and exercise. Physical fitness is essential to building strong spiritual resistance. If you're not in good physical shape, you won't be able to block out negative spiritual vibrations.

Sometimes gaining weight can help you repel negative spiritual influences. When you grow spiritually, your growth can manifest outwardly, too. As your mind becomes stronger and you start to overcome difficulties, your physical body develops accordingly, and you become well built. A richness of mind can manifest as a robust body. Often, the bigger your body gets, the more resistance you have against negative spirits. In this sense, being at your ideal body weight may not necessarily be ideal for your mind.

Those who are constantly suffering from spiritual disturbances fret over every little thing, and these people have difficulty putting on weight. If you are experiencing spiritual disturbances or feel that you are under the influence of an evil spirit, one way to repel them is to gain weight. From my own experience, if you gain one kilogram (two pounds) you will gain the strength to cast off one spirit. An extra five kilograms (ten pounds) will let you cast off five spirits. So if you are underweight and feel weak, I suggest that you gain five kilograms, and you'll start to feel more confident and tolerant. You may be surprised by how effective gaining weight is for repelling evil spirits. One last thing I would like to note is that simply gaining weight may cause lifestyle diseases, so be sure to work out regularly as you put on weight.

6

Meditation for People with Dementia

Question:

I have a grandmother who has been suffering from senile dementia for the past three years. How can we help people like her, who lack cognitive abilities due to illness, practice introspective meditation so that they will awaken to their divine nature?˝

Answer:

I don't think your grandmother is in a condition to practice meditation, because patients suffering from senile dementia have difficulty concentrating the mind. In this case, either you or other members of her family need to practice meditation for her, and the type of meditation I recommend would be meditation to harmonize an interpersonal relationship. Set aside a certain time every day to concentrate your mind and vividly visualize your grandmother quickly recovering her health and living happily and harmoniously with everyone. This will become the source of energy to heal her.

In the spirit world, thought is everything; what we think manifests instantaneously. This is a law of the spirit world. Our thoughts often do not immediately become reality in this world because we reside in physical bodies, which limit our spiritual capabilities. Still, the same spiritual law applies to those of us living in this third-dimensional, material world, because this world is not completely cut off from the multidimensional spirit world, which consists of the worlds of the fourth dimension and beyond. This physical world we live in actually coexists with the world of higher dimensions. So the laws of the spirit world are also at work in the physical world. But since we are constrained by the flow of time in this world, it requires a certain amount of time for our thoughts to manifest, and we may have to go through many twists and turns along the way. So one way you and your family can help your grandmother recover is to clearly visualize her living with good health and in harmony with everyone so that your vision may become reality.

Another way is to look into the cause of her dementia. Why did this happen to her? While senile dementia is sometimes caused by physical problems, it is also often caused by spiritual possession. Those who have opened the windows of their mind become especially vulnerable to negative spiritual influences and so are prone to spiritual possession. In the case of your grandmother, I sense that she has been influenced and possessed by several negative spirits.

Spiritual possession usually stems from negative thoughts and feelings. The most effective way to remove the possessing spirits is to look within one's mind and reflect on and correct any wrong thoughts, but in cases like your grandmother's, in which people lack the cognitive ability to engage in self-reflection on their own, someone else needs to do it for them.

Do you think that the cause of your grandmother's dementia could relate to her family members? Is it possible that you have something to do with her illness, too? Please ponder these questions and consider whether you or other members of the family might have caused her illness. If you find that disharmony or conflicts in the family might have caused her dementia, repent them, and remove the causes one by one. When loved ones' physical condition prohibits them from making sound judgments, those close to them need to do the work on their behalf.

Another way to help is to dispel darkness by increasing and strengthening the light. Darkness in your home and darkness inside you often trigger spiritual possession. So my advice is to increase your inner light until you have sufficient light to illuminate others. Drive away the darkness with an overwhelming amount of light, an overwhelming sense of good will, and the overwhelming force of hope. I hope that you will start living with this in mind.

7

On Reflection and Letting Go of the Past

Question:

When I practice self-reflection, sometimes I am not sure whether I am doing it right. I think you said that God gave us the power to reflect on and correct our mistakes out of His mercy but that, at the same time, God expects us to forget the past. Could you tell us about when to repent and when to let go of our mistakes and move on?

Answer:

That's a good question. I think it is very difficult to tell when to repent and when to let go of our mistakes, because it largely depends on the circumstances of each individual. Those who mainly teach self-reflection would simply tell everyone to reflect on their thoughts and actions regardless of what their situation is. It is true that self-reflection is one of the safest ways to attaining enlightenment. We are less likely to go the wrong way if we start our spiritual practice with self-reflection.

Those who seek self-realization or practice positive thinking are prone to going the wrong way when their minds are clouded by their egos. If you practice positive thinking only for your own benefit and stay blind to your own faults, you may end up harming others unknowingly. This is why the balance between a progressive, future-oriented mindset and a self-reflective mindset has long been a topic of discussion.

First, I would like to talk about forgetting or letting go of your mistakes. No matter how much we reflect on ourselves, we may sometimes keep feeling miserable and unable to find a way out. We may find ourselves caught in a negative cycle of endless repentance.

Suppose that the company you work for is in financial trouble and is facing a crisis. Layoffs resulting from corporate downsizing and union protests against the layoffs are rocking the company. You hold an important position in the company— perhaps you are a union chair or a board member of the company's management team. You know that hundreds if not thousands of people could lose their jobs, so you want to do something to help the situation, but it is simply beyond your ability. You feel powerless because there is nothing you can do to save them from losing their jobs. The company remains in a state of havoc for six months and eventually goes under, forcing everyone to go their separate ways, and now you occasionally hear the bad news of their sufferings. You may reflect back on your responsibility as the union chair or board member and repent the mistakes you made but find yourself trapped in a cycle of repentance for five or ten years and unable to get out of it.

If you find yourself in a situation like this, you need to know that there are certain things in life that you cannot control. Being human, we only have limited power as to what we can do, and repentance sometimes does not get you out of the situation you are in. It is true that our thoughts will eventually become reality, and so our circumstances are a manifestation of the state of our mind. But our life can make a complete shift and change course when a lot of people get involved. We sometimes helplessly get tossed about and embroiled in the tidal waves of life. And some of us cannot forgive ourselves for this, even decades later.

When you get trapped in a cycle of self-blame, I suggest that you put your memories aside until you can build yourself up again. You don't have to completely forget what happened, but try to gain some emotional distance from it. Instead of dragging the past around with you, become a new you and start fresh. Break out of the cycle of self-blame, and search for the goodness inside you. Find the shining self within, and focus on becoming a new you.

After some time has passed, you can reflect on your mistakes again with fresh eyes. When you reexamine yourself and look back on your past from this new perspective, you will be able to discover the mistakes that you and other people involved made and better understand what everyone should have done. You may find things out about yourself that you hadn't realized and contemplate them more deeply.

If you come to understand mistakes that others made, you can learn from their mistakes and apply them in your own life.

If you cannot change what has already happened, don't let it cause you present suffering and distress. You need to let go of your past mistakes, because dragging them around will sap your motivation to continue improving and advancing and instead will keep you wandering around in the darkness. You need to have the courage to cut yourself off from the past mistakes that are creating darkness inside you.

This all might sound too abstract, so let me share the experience that first made me contemplate this topic. I used to work for a trading company while doing the kind of spiritual work I do now. I tried to keep my spiritual work secret from my coworkers, but it somehow leaked out. Since I didn't offer any explanation about the rumor, people started saying whatever they thought I was doing and dressed up the story, which put me in a difficult position.

Because I had published a book under the title *The Spiritual Messages of Nichiren*, word spread in the company that I was a leader of the Japanese religious movement Soka Gakkai (which was originally based on Nichiren Buddhism). Some people said that I performed exorcisms with the same kind of large paper shaker that Shinto priests use in their purification rites. One rumor was that I had collapsed, frothing at the mouth, while I was performing this rite. There were any numbers of stories like that. It was amazing how the stories changed completely as they passed from person to person.

It all started when I shared with a couple of people my experience of opening the window of my mind to the spirit world. I told these people because they were aware of the existence of the spirit world and wanted to hear about my experience. They got so inspired by my story that they passionately told other people, who were suspicious of my experience. Although the people I directly talked to thought that it was a wonderful experience that should be shared, those who heard it from them did not feel the same way. The more people believed in what I said, the more peculiar they appeared to others.

So people who heard my experiences indirectly from others started spreading a lot of rumors. They said that I had become the leader of a certain religious group, that I had collapsed while performing a purification rite, or that I had lost my mind when I was transferred to the New York office.

While all this was happening, I thoroughly checked to see if I had done something wrong to cause this situation. But ultimately, the problem was because I wasn't doing the work I was meant to do. If my main career had been spiritual work, even if some people criticized me, others would have recognized the value of the work I had done. But I took a bashing because spiritual work was not my main job at the time.

The people who spoke ill of me were simply ignorant of the Truths. It was practically impossible for me to share all the Truths I'd discovered with the people in the business world. It felt as if a thorn was stuck in my heart. It was the pain of not being able to explain; it was the pain of not being understood. I tried to remove that thorn by reflecting on my thoughts and actions, but I just couldn't resolve it, no matter how much I tried. The only way to get over it was to show my true self, but my circumstances didn't allow me to do so at the time. This kind of dilemma cannot be resolved by self-reflection, because we cannot change other people's values. The only way out was to start doing what I was meant to do and carry out my mission as a religious leader. But I also knew that it would take some time for me to do that.

Even though I wanted to explain what was really happening to me—that I was not a guru or leader of any group and that I hadn't lost my mind while I was in New York—I was not in a position to convince them that they were misunderstanding things.

I hadn't done anything wrong, but my coworkers were not bad people, either—they simply weren't aware of the truth. I realized that there was nothing I could do at that time and that only time would solve my problem. I decided to put up with the criticism for the time being and let Lethe, the river of oblivion, wash away my past; I decided to let go and forget about it. I cut myself off from all the shackles of criticism and focused on rebuilding myself. I decided that I would reflect on what had happened once I achieved a higher state of awareness and could see the world in a positive light.

Years have passed since I left that job and started walking the path of Truth. Now, when I think back on what happened, I have no negative feelings about the people who spoke behind my back and spread rumors. And when I look within, I find no wounds or scars in my heart, because I had gained the inner strength to let their words go. Without having built this inner strength, I would have gotten stuck in a

181

cycle of endless repentance while letting the criticism hurt me.

Anguishing over how we can improve our image or gain others' understanding will not help us escape from the negative loop. We need to turn our back on these kinds of events and set out toward the bright future to fulfill a higher mission. Instead of seeking understanding from the people around us, we should focus on what we can do on our own to elevate ourselves to a higher level of awareness. With this higher perspective, we will be able to see events in a different light.

Currently, many people are helping my organization, Happy Science, but both volunteers and staff may sometimes face criticism from their acquaintances, relatives, and colleagues when they find out about their involvement with Happy Science. But they won't necessarily be able to find the cause of this criticism within themselves. At the same time, we can't say that the fault lies completely with those who are doing the criticizing. Their misunderstanding might be caused by the negative stereotypes about religious organizations in today's society. They may be prejudiced simply because of what they were taught, and so they may not be the ones to be blamed for their negative view.

If you face a situation like this, take courage and let go of the small self that wants others' approval and wants to avoid criticism. Strengthen your inner light and resolve to live for a higher mission. You will then be able to transcend the boundaries of your limited self and discover the true self that you weren't able to see when you were reflecting on your mistakes.

As Wumen Huikai suggests in his koan "The Enlightened Man" in his book *The Gateless Gate*, we humans carry immense power within us, but we have a tendency to limit ourselves.* We bind ourselves with various social norms and the opinions of others, including our siblings, parents, relatives, friends, and teachers. It's as if we swathe ourselves in an invisible string of can'ts, don'ts, and shouldn'ts. If we try to reflect on our mistakes while our hands are bound by this string of limitation, we may only get further entangled in it. There are times when we have to just cut the thread; we need to cut ourselves off from the self that keeps blaming ourselves or feeling guilty about our failures. Free yourself from

183

---

* A koan is a question, dialogue, story, or statement used in Zen practice to contemplate and deepen one's enlightenment. "The Enlightened Man" is the twentieth koan in Wumen Huikai's *The Gateless Gate*. Refer to *The Laws of the Sun*, pages 210-212 (IRH Press: New York, 2012).

the negative thoughts that bind you, and rediscover your original, unlimited self.

Another koan in *The Gateless Gate* tells a story of a man hanging on to the branch of a tree by his teeth. Someone approaches and asks him, "Why did Bodhidharma come from the West?" This question is asking about the intention of Bodhidharma, the founder of the Zen sect, to come from India to China to teach the essence of Zen to Eka, who inherited Bodhidharma's mantle. There was a rule that said that any Buddhist practitioner who entered the path of discipline must answer when asked this question. But if the hanging man tries to answer the question, he will have to open his mouth and will fall from the tree. And unfortunately, he is not allowed to use his hands to hang from the branch. But if he does not answer this question, he will be disqualified as a Buddhist practitioner. So he is caught in a dilemma between not being able to open his mouth and not being able to answer the question.

We often face situations like this in life. We may feel that we are faced with a dilemma, when in fact we are simply binding ourselves with the rules we have set ourselves. We have to ask ourselves if the premises upon which we are basing our decision are correct.

In the story of the man hanging from the tree, for example, we have to ask if it is really correct to presume that Buddhist practitioners must always answer the question about why Bodhidharma came from the West. What entitles the man who asks the question to disqualify the monk when he cannot use his mouth to answer the question? Why isn't the hanging monk allowed to use his hands instead of his mouth? These conditions are all presupposed as if they are unchangeable rules. But we have to question the validity of such assumptions.

We humans, especially those with a religious inclination, often tie ourselves up with conventional doctrines and dogmas that tell us what we must and must not do. And like the monk hanging on to a tree branch by his teeth, we allow ourselves to get entangled and paralyzed by these conditions while still trying to force ourselves to find the mistakes in our mind.

We often corner ourselves with rules of our own making, but we must break through this shell and regain a powerful self. When we go beyond the boundaries of how we see ourselves—not as a five- or six-foot-tall physical being, but as a bigger existence of fifteen to thirty feet or more—we start seeing the world and its people in a new light. Don't let others or outside circumstances sway you. Take a step forward to build a brighter future. Only then can you go beyond the boundaries of self-reflection and start seeing things from a broader perspective.

We can certainly cleanse our mistakes and sins from our soul through self-reflection, but this doesn't mean that self-reflection is the only way out. When we believe that we must repent our mistakes to solve any problem that we face, we may find ourselves caught in a dilemma like the monk's: obliged to answer a question while we are, figuratively speaking, hanging on to a tree branch with our teeth.

It is true that what happens in the outer world is a projection of our inner world. However, when you bind yourself to this principle—in other words, if you think that your mind is the cause of all the problems you face—you may start seeing yourself as a sinner. Occasionally we need to consider whether we are practicing self-reflection correctly.

Unshackle and release the person of immense power within. Nullify all the preconditions that you believe you need to fulfill, such as not being able to use your hands or having to answer the question. Ask yourself whether such preconditions are valid in every situation. You may sometimes find that these rules are entirely unnecessary.

Suppose a thug starts assaulting me, saying that everything I say is wrong and threatening to kill me because he believes I am causing harm to humanity. Since I am a man of religion, he may expect me to adhere to Gandhi's principle of absolute nonresistance to violence and surrender. But I would probably fight back. I would not bind myself with the principle of nonresistance if my life were in danger.

We should not let our inaction worsen a situation. When we are in emergency situations, we have to step out of our own limiting notions of what a person of religion is supposed to do. Limiting ourselves with these stereotypical images may actually hold us back and allow others to commit mistakes that we could have prevented. So occasionally, we need to be flexible. Breaking out of the preconceived ideas that bind us can manifest in the form of justice. This is one aspect of justice that can help us forge a new path.

Those who have acquired the habit of reflecting on their mistakes and failures tend to blame themselves for everything. Generally speaking, it is good to understand your role in the problems you face, but taking the blame for everything may actually inhibit the growth of others. For example, people working under you may make mistakes. You may be tempted to take responsibility for their mistakes, thinking that everything that happens to you is a manifestation of your thoughts. But rather than mulling over the situation, it is more effective to just tell them straight out to fix their mistakes and give instructions on how to do their job properly. Your problem is solved the moment you tell your subordinates that they are not doing their job right and that they should follow a certain procedure. You can even give more specific directions as to what needs to be done in the morning and what in the afternoon, or what to look out for in a certain process.

People who tend to take all the blame may instead contemplate the reasons their subordinates have acted in a way that has obviously damaged the business. They may feel that they need to take the time to lead by example so that their subordinates will eventually pick up on their mistakes. But this kind of attitude may only bring about a negative impact on the company's overall performance—while the boss is agonizing over the employee's mistake, the employee remains entirely oblivious to the problem. It's better for everyone if the boss just comes right out and says that the subordinate has made a mistake and needs to fix it. If saying it outright is hard, the boss can write the subordinate a quick note instead. As this example shows, weakheartedness lets us drag our suffering around with us and bring trouble to others. So the risk of focusing on self-reflection is that it can turn us into good-natured but weakhearted people.

Making a habit of reflecting on your mistakes is fine, but you need to occasionally check whether you have become a good-natured but weakhearted person. If you think that you have, you may need to draw a line, let go of your past mistakes, and focus on elevating yourself to a higher level. When you review your mistakes later from a higher perspective, you will be able to see things that you didn't notice before. You may be able to find an entirely new way of solving problems. Sometimes you just have to think big and think outside the box, as Ryoma Sakamoto* did.

In your meditation, liberate yourself to make yourself bigger or smaller at will. There is no reason why your soul should remain the same size as your physical body. Free your mind and let your soul become as big as a giant or as small as a fairy. This

---

* Ryoma Sakamoto (1836–1867) was a leader of the Meiji Restoration movement, which peacefully restored power to the emperor from the Tokugawa shogunate and ushered in a new era of modernization and prosperity in Japan.

complete freedom of the soul, which lets us sometimes reflect on our thoughts and feelings and at
other times lets go of negative feelings, leads us to
understand the spiritual laws of meditation.

Afterword

How did you feel about this book, *The Miracle of Meditation*? Did it make you feel that meditation is something you can incorporate into your daily life? Did it help you understand what it means to concentrate your mind and how doing so can improve your life and promote your spiritual growth? Did it motivate you to pursue meditation more seriously?

If you are interested in continuing your study or practice of meditation, we offer programs and guidance on introspection and various meditation practices at my organization, Happy Science.

It is my sincere hope that this book will offer many people a chance to experience the mystical miracles of meditation.

Ryuho Okawa
Founder and CEO
Happy Science Group

The contents of this book were compiled from translations of the following works by Ryuho Okawa:

Chapter 1: The Secrets of Meditation
"Meisou No Gokui." Chapter 1 in *Meisou No Gokui*.
Tokyo: IRH Press Co., Ltd. 1989.
"Meisou No Gokui Kougi." Chapter 2 in *Meisou No Gokui*.
Tokyo: IRH Press Co., Ltd. 1989.

Chapter 2: Meditations for Happiness
"Koufuku Meisou Hou Kougi." Chapter 4 in *Meisou No Gokui*.
Tokyo: IRH Press Co., Ltd. 1989.

Meditation to Become One with Nature:
Excerpt from "Mui Shizen No Meisou."
Chapter 3 in *Okawa Ryuho Reigen Zenshuu Bekkan 3*.
Tokyo: Happy Science, 2008.

Contemplation on Finding Contentment:
Excerpt from
"Hansei Shuuhou 1 Tarukoto O Shiranu Yokubou Wa Naika."
Jissen Hansei Hou. Compact disc.
Happy Science, 1996.

Visualizing Relationship Harmony:
Excerpt from "Taijin Kankei Chouwa No Meisou." Chapter 5
in *Okawa Ryuho Reigen Zenshuu Bekkan 3*.
Tokyo: Happy Science, 2008.

Chapter 3: Q&A on Meditation
Q1, Q2, Q6, Q7: "Koufuku Meisou Hou Shitsugi Outou." Chapter 5
in *Meisou No Gokui*. Tokyo: IRH Press Co., Ltd. 1989.

Q3, Q4, Q5: "Meisou No Gokui Shitsugi Outou." Chapter 3
in *Meisou No Gokui*. Tokyo: IRH Press Co., Ltd. 1989.

About the Author

RYUHO OKAWA is a global visionary, renowned spiritual leader, and best-selling author in Japan with a simple goal: to help people find true happiness and create a better world.

His deep compassion and sense of responsibility for the happiness of each individual has prompted him to publish over 2,000 titles of religious, spiritual, and self-development teachings, covering a broad range of topics including how our thoughts influence reality, the nature of love, and the path to enlightenment. He also writes on the topics of management and economy, as well as the relationship between religion and politics in the global context. To date, Okawa's books have sold over 100 million copies worldwide and been translated into 28 languages.

Okawa has dedicated himself to improving society and creating a better world. In 1986, Okawa founded Happy Science as a spiritual movement dedicated to bringing greater happiness to humankind by uniting religions and cultures to live in harmony. Happy Science has grown rapidly from its beginnings in

Japan to a worldwide organization with over 10 million members. Okawa is compassionately committed to the spiritual growth of others. In addition to writing and publishing books, he continues to give lectures around the world.

About Happy Science

Happy Science is a global movement that empowers individuals to find purpose and spiritual happiness and to share that happiness with their families, societies, and the world. With more than twelve million members around the world, Happy Science aims to increase awareness of spiritual truths and expand our capacity for love, compassion, and joy so that together we can create the kind of world we all wish to live in.

Activities at Happy Science are based on the Principles of Happiness (Love, Wisdom, Self-Reflection, and Progress). These principles embrace worldwide philosophies and beliefs, transcending boundaries of culture and religions.

The Principles of Happiness

Love teaches us to give ourselves freely without expecting anything in return; it encompasses giving, nurturing, and forgiveness.

Wisdom leads us to the insights of spiritual truths, and opens us to the true meaning of life and the will of God (the universe, the highest power, Eternal Buddha).

Self-Reflection brings a mindful, nonjudgmental lens to our thoughts and actions to help us find our truest selves—the essence of our souls—and deepen our connection to the highest power. It helps us attain a clean and peaceful mind and leads us to the right life path.

Progress emphasizes the positive, dynamic aspects of our spiritual growth—actions we can take to manifest and spread happiness around the world. It's a path that not only expands our soul growth, but also furthers the collective potential of the world we live in.

Programs and Events

The doors of Happy Science are open to all. We offer a variety of programs and events, including self-exploration and self-growth programs, spiritual seminars, meditation and contemplation sessions, study groups, and book events.

Various meditation programs are available at your nearest Happy Science location including the following:

- Four Stage Meditation (Flowing Stream, Floating Clouds, Full Moon, Communication with Heaven)
- The Eightfold Path Seminar
- Gratitude to Parents Reflection Seminar
- A Dialogue with Your Guardian Spirit

International Seminars

Each year, friends from all over the world join our international seminars, held at our faith centers in Japan. Different programs are offered each year and cover a wide variety of topics, including improving relationships, practicing the Eightfold Path to enlightenment, and loving yourself, to name just a few.

Happy Science Monthly

Our monthly publication covers the latest featured lectures, members' life-changing experiences and other news from members around the world, book reviews, and many other topics. Downloadable PDF files are available at happyscience-na.org. Copies and back issues in Portuguese, Chinese, and other languages are available upon request. For more information, contact us via e-mail at tokyo@happy-science.org.

Contact Information

Happy Science is a worldwide organization with faith centers around the globe. For a comprehensive list of centers, visit the worldwide directory at happy-science.org or happyscience-na.org. The following are some of the many Happy Science locations:

United States and Canada

New York
79 Franklin Street
New York, NY 10013
Phone: 212-343-7972
Fax: 212-343-7973
Email: ny@happy-science.org
website: newyork.happyscience-na.org

Los Angeles
1590 E. Del Mar Blvd.
Pasadena, CA 91106
Phone: 626-395-7775
Fax: 626-395-7776
Email: la@happy-science.org
website: losangeles.happyscience-na.org

Orange County
10231 Slater Ave #204
Fountain Valley, CA 92708
Phone: 714-745-1140
Email: oc@happy-science.org

San Diego
Email: sandiego@happy-science.org

San Francisco
525 Clinton Street
Redwood City, CA 94062
Phone/Fax: 650-363-2777
Email: sf@happy-science.org
website: sanfrancisco.happyscience-na.org

Florida
5208 8th St.
Zephyrhills, FL 33542
Phone: 813-715-0000
Fax: 813-715-0010
Email: florida@happy-science.org
website: florida.happyscience-na.org

New Jersey
725 River Rd. #102B
Edgewater, NJ 07025
Phone: 201-313-0127
Fax: 201-313-0120
Email: nj@happy-science.org
website: newjersey.happyscience-na.org

Atlanta

1874 Piedmont Ave. NE
Suite 360-C
Atlanta, GA 30324
Phone: 404-892-7770
Email: atlanta@happy-science.org
website: atlanta.happyscience-na.org

Hawaii

1221 Kapiolani Blvd., Suite 920
Honolulu, HI 96814
Phone: 808-591-9772
Fax: 808-591-9776
Email: hi@happy-science.org
website: hawaii.happyscience-na.org

Kauai

4504 Kukui Street
Dragon Building Suite 21
Kapaa, HI 96746
Phone: 808-822-7007
Fax: 808-822-6007
Email: kauai-hi@happy-science.org
website: happyscience-kauai.org

Toronto

323 College Street,
Toronto, ON M5T 1S2
Canada
Phone/Fax: 1-416-901-3747
Email: toronto@happy-science.org
website: happyscience-na.org

Vancouver

#212-2609 East 49th Avenue
Vancouver, V5S 1J9
Canada
Phone: 1-604-437-7735
Fax: 1-604-437-7764
Email: vancouver@happy-science.org
website: happyscience-na.org

International

Tokyo

1-6-7 Togoshi
Shinagawa, Tokyo, 142-0041
Japan
Phone: 81-3-6384-5770
Fax: 81-3-6384-5776
Email: tokyo@happy-science.org
website: happy-science.org

London

3 Margaret Street,
London, W1W 8RE
United Kingdom
Phone: 44-20-7323-9255
Fax: 44-20-7323-9344
Email: eu@happy-science.org
website: happyscience-uk.org

Sydney
516 Pacific Hwy
Lane Cove North,
2066 NSW
Australia
Phone: 61-2-9411-2877
Fax: 61-2-9411-2822
Email: aus@happy-science.org
website: happyscience.org.au

Brazil Headquarters
Rua. Domingos de Morais 1154,
Vila Mariana, Sao Paulo,
CEP 04009-002
Brazil
Phone: 55-11-5088-3800
Fax: 55-11-5088-3806
Email: sp@happy-science.org
website: cienciadafelicidade.com.br

Jundlal
Rua Congo, 447,
Jd.Bonfiglioli, Jundiai- CEP
13207 - 340
Phone: 55-11-4587-5952
Email: jundiai@happy-sciece.org

Seoul
74, Sadang-ro 27-gil,
Dongjak-gu, Seoul, Korea
Phone: 82-2-3478-8777
Fax: 82-2-3478-9777
Email: korea@happy-science.org
website: happyscience-korea.org

Taipei
No. 89, Lane 155, Dunhua N. Road
Songshan District
Taipei City 105
Taiwan
Phone: 886-2-2719-9377
Fax: 886-2-2719-5570
Email: taiwan@happy-science.org
website: happyscience-tw.org

Malaysia
No 22A, Block2, Jalil Link
Jalan Jalil Jaya 2, Bukit Jalil
57000, Kuala Lumpur
Malaysia
Phone: 60-3-8998-7877
Fax: 60-3-8998-7977
Email: Malaysia@happy-science.org
Website: happyscience.org.my

Kathmandu
Kathmandu Metropolitan City,
Ward No. 15, Ring Road, Kimdol,
Sitapaila,Kathmandu
Nepal
Phone: 97-714-272931
Email: ncpal@happy-science.org
           nepaltrainingcenter@happy-
           science.org

Uganda
Plot 877 Rubaga Road Kampala
P.O. Box 34130
Kampala, Uganda
Phone: 256-79-3238-002
Email: uganda@happy-science.org

About IRH Press USA Inc.

IRH Press USA Inc. was founded in 2013 as an affiliated firm of IRH Press Co., Ltd. Based in New York, the press publishes books in various categories including spirituality, religion, and self-improvement and publishes books by Ryuho Okawa, the author of 100 million books sold worldwide. For more information, visit OkawaBooks.com.

Follow us on:
Facebook: MasterOkawaBooks
Twitter: OkawaBooks
Goodreads: RyuhoOkawa
Instagram: OkawaBooks
Pinterest: OkawaBooks

Books by Ryuho Okawa

THE ESSENCE of BUDDHA
The Path to Enlightenment

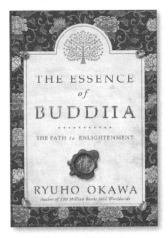

Softcover · 208 pages
ISBN: 978-1942125-06-8
$14.95

By offering a new perspective on core Buddhist thoughts that have long been cloaked in mystique, Okawa brings these teachings to life for modern people. *The Essence of Buddha* distills a way of life that anyone can practice to achieve a life of self-growth, compassionate living, and true happiness.

INVITATION to HAPPINESS
7 Inspirations from Your Inner Angel

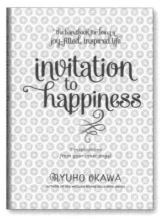

Hardcover · 176 pages
ISBN: 978-1-942125-01-3
$16.99

In this book, you will find all the tools you need to live more confidently, peacefully, and authentically, including practices for introspection, brief guided visualizations, tips and hints for contemplation, and even a discovery journal area to record inspirations from your inner angel. Through reading, contemplating and writing—you will find simple step-by-step action plans that serve as a path to the truest self—allowing you to live a more confident, connected life of inner peace.

THE LAWS OF JUSTICE
How We Can Solve World Conflicts and Bring Peace

THE HEART OF WORK
10 Keys to Living Your Calling

THINK BIG!
Be Positive and Be Brave to Achieve Your Dreams

MESSAGES FROM HEAVEN
What Jesus, Buddha, Muhammad, and Moses Would Say Today

THE LAWS OF THE SUN
One Source, One Planet, One People

SECRETS OF THE EVERLASTING TRUTHS
A New Paradigm for Living on Earth

THE NINE DIMENSIONS
Unveiling the Laws of Eternity

THE MOMENT OF TRUTH
Become a Living Angel Today

CHANGE YOUR LIFE, CHANGE THE WORLD
A Spiritual Guide to Living Now

207

For a complete list of books, visit OkawaBooks.com.